ESPECIALLY FOR

_____

FROM

_____

DATE

_____

© 2016 by Barbour Publishing

Written and compiled by Karin Dahl Silver.

Print ISBN 978-1-64352-915-8

All scripture quotations are taken from the King James Version of the Bible.

Published by Barbour Books, an imprint of Barbour Publishing, Inc., 1810 Barbour Drive, Uhrichsville, Ohio 44683, www.barbourbooks.com

Our mission is to inspire the world with the life-changing message of the Bible.

Member of the
Evangelical Christian
Publishers Association

Printed in the United States of America.

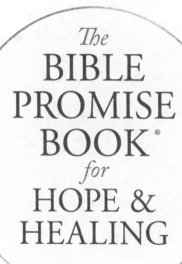

The
BIBLE PROMISE BOOK®
for
HOPE & HEALING

BARBOUR BOOKS
An Imprint of Barbour Publishing, Inc.

CONTENTS

INTRODUCTION

Whatever the need of the moment, the answer can be found in scripture—if we take the time to search for it. Whatever we're feeling, whatever we're suffering, whatever we're hoping, the Bible has something to say to us.

This collection of devotional thoughts and Bible verses is meant for use as a handy reference when you need the Bible's guidance and encouragement on a particular problem in your life. It is not meant to replace regular Bible study or the use of a concordance for in-depth study of a subject. There are many facets of your life and many topics in the Bible that are not covered here.

But if, for example, you are struggling with depression or loneliness, shame or trials, some of the Bible's promises are available to you in these pages. You'll find carefully selected verses for dozens of topics dealing with hope and healing, arranged alphabetically for ease of use.

We hope it will be an encouragement to you as you read.

ABUSE

Abuse, in whatever form it takes, is completely against God's just and loving nature. His Word speaks out repeatedly against the wickedness of oppression—harming others with violent actions and words. An abuse survivor has a long, difficult road to walk, but your God will go with you—no amount of pain you carry is too difficult for Him. He invites you to pour out your heart; He can fill you with His truth and peace to answer the shame and guilt you might feel. These Bible promises show that the almighty God is powerful to defend and restore you.

The LORD also will be a refuge for the oppressed,
a refuge in times of trouble. And they that know thy
name will put their trust in thee: for thou, LORD,
hast not forsaken them that seek thee.

PSALM 9:9–10

*Humble yourselves therefore under the mighty
hand of God, that he may exalt you in due time:
casting all your care upon him; for he careth for you.*
1 PETER 5:6–7

*I sought the Lord, and he heard me, and delivered
me from all my fears. They looked unto him, and were
lightened: and their faces were not ashamed.*
PSALM 34:4–5

*When my father and my mother forsake me,
then the LORD will take me up.*
PSALM 27:10

*I will say of the LORD, He is my refuge and
my fortress: my God; in him will I trust.*
PSALM 91:2

*Be ye angry, and sin not: let not the sun go down
upon your wrath: neither give place to the devil.*

EPHESIANS 4:26–27

*Likewise the Spirit also helpeth our infirmities:
for we know not what we should pray for as we
ought: but the Spirit itself maketh intercession
for us with groanings which cannot be uttered.
And he that searcheth the hearts knoweth
what is the mind of the Spirit, because he
maketh intercession for the saints
according to the will of God.*

ROMANS 8:26–27

*Strengthen ye the weak hands, and confirm the
feeble knees. Say to them that are of a fearful heart,
Be strong, fear not: behold, your God will come
with vengeance, even God with a recompence;
he will come and save you.*

ISAIAH 35:3–4

For whatsoever is born of God overcometh the world:
and this is the victory that overcometh the world,
even our faith. Who is he that overcometh the world,
but he that believeth that Jesus is the Son of God?
1 JOHN 5:4–5

The LORD bless thee, and keep thee: the LORD
make his face shine upon thee, and be gracious
unto thee: the LORD lift up his countenance
upon thee, and give thee peace.
NUMBERS 6:24–26

But they that wait upon the Lord shall renew
their strength; they shall mount up with wings
as eagles; they shall run, and not be weary;
and they shall walk, and not faint.
ISAIAH 40:31

And I will restore to you the years that the locust hath eaten, the cankerworm, and the caterpiller, and the palmerworm, my great army which I sent among you. And ye shall eat in plenty, and be satisfied, and praise the name of the LORD your God, that hath dealt wondrously with you: and my people shall never be ashamed.

JOEL 2:25–26

A father of the fatherless, and a judge of the widows, is God in his holy habitation. God setteth the solitary in families: he bringeth out those which are bound with chains: but the rebellious dwell in a dry land.

PSALM 68:5–6

For thou hast been a strength to the poor, a strength to the needy in his distress, a refuge from the storm, a shadow from the heat, when the blast of the terrible ones is as a storm against the wall.

ISAIAH 25:4

ADDICTION

For those who struggle with overcoming addiction, take heart in these truths. Our God is stronger than anything that holds power over us. No matter how far we fall, God can always reach down to us and lift us up. His grace and forgiveness are greater than any amount of temptation or relapses we might experience. The Almighty is near and ready to help. These Bible promises show that Jesus has already won the victory over anything that entangles us. Moving forward in His freedom, we can learn to love and worship Him with all our hearts and our strength.

If the Son therefore shall make you free,
ye shall be free indeed.
JOHN 8:36

Stand fast therefore in the liberty wherewith
Christ hath made us free, and be not entangled
again with the yoke of bondage.
GALATIANS 5:1

The Spirit of the Lord GOD is upon me; because the LORD hath anointed me to preach good tidings unto the meek; he hath sent me to bind up the brokenhearted, to proclaim liberty to the captives, and the opening of the prison to them that are bound.

ISAIAH 61:1

Knowing this, that our old man is crucified with him, that the body of sin might be destroyed, that henceforth we should not serve sin. For he that is dead is freed from sin. For in that he died, he died unto sin once: but in that he liveth, he liveth unto God.

ROMANS 6:6–7, 10

There hath no temptation taken you but such as is common to man: but God is faithful, who will not suffer you to be tempted above that ye are able; but will with the temptation also make a way to escape, that ye may be able to bear it.

1 CORINTHIANS 10:13

Dearly beloved, I beseech you as strangers and pilgrims, abstain from fleshly lusts, which war against the soul.

1 PETER 2:11

I beseech you therefore, brethren, by the mercies of God,
that ye present your bodies a living sacrifice, holy,
acceptable unto God, which is your reasonable service.
Romans 12:1

But I see another law in my members, warring against the
law of my mind, and bringing me into captivity to the law
of sin which is in my members. O wretched man that I am!
who shall deliver me from the body of this death?
I thank God through Jesus Christ our Lord.
Romans 7:23–25

Forasmuch then as Christ hath suffered for us in
the flesh, arm yourselves likewise with the same mind:
for he that hath suffered in the flesh hath ceased from sin;
that he no longer should live the rest of his time in the flesh
to the lusts of men, but to the will of God. For the time past
of our life may suffice us to have wrought the will of the
Gentiles, when we walked in lasciviousness, lusts, excess of
wine, revellings, banquetings, and abominable idolatries:
wherein they think it strange that ye run not with them to
the same excess of riot, speaking evil of you: who shall give
account to him that is ready to judge the quick and the dead.
1 Peter 4:1–5

This I say then, Walk in the Spirit, and ye shall not fulfil the lust of the flesh. For the flesh lusteth against the Spirit, and the Spirit against the flesh: and these are contrary the one to the other: so that ye cannot do the things that ye would. And they that are Christ's have crucified the flesh with the affections and lusts.

GALATIANS 5:16–17, 24

All things are lawful unto me, but all things are not expedient: all things are lawful for me, but I will not be brought under the power of any.

1 CORINTHIANS 6:12

Let not sin therefore reign in your mortal body, that ye should obey it in the lusts thereof. Neither yield ye your members as instruments of unrighteousness unto sin: but yield yourselves unto God, as those that are alive from the dead, and your members as instruments of righteousness unto God. For sin shall not have dominion over you: for ye are not under the law, but under grace.

ROMANS 6:12–14

ANGER

On our healing journey, we might have a million reasons to be angry. We're furious at people who have hurt us deeply. We grow frustrated at our bodies' slow healing or the onslaught of bad news from our doctors. While anger burns bright, its heat cannot heal. Anger can quickly reduce our hearts to ashes and cultivate a rich growing place for bitterness. God can help us with the anger we feel. He is gracious to listen, to forgive, and to work peace within us. These Bible promises show that though anger is powerful, God's healing can overcome its harm.

I am crucified with Christ: nevertheless I live; yet not I, but Christ liveth in me: and the life which I now live in the flesh I live by the faith of the Son of God, who loved me, and gave himself for me.

GALATIANS 2:20

[Charity] doth not behave itself unseemly, seeketh not her own, is not easily provoked, thinketh no evil; rejoiceth not in iniquity, but rejoiceth in the truth; beareth all things, believeth all things, hopeth all things, endureth all things.

1 CORINTHIANS 13:5–7

Be ye angry, and sin not: let not the sun go down upon your wrath: neither give place to the devil.

EPHESIANS 4:26–27

Looking diligently lest any man fail of the grace of God; lest any root of bitterness springing up trouble you, and thereby many be defiled.

HEBREWS 12:15

Cease from anger, and forsake wrath: fret not thyself in any wise to do evil. For evildoers shall be cut off: but those that wait upon the Lord, they shall inherit the earth.

PSALM 37:8–9

Being confident of this very thing, that he which hath begun a good work in you will perform it until the day of Jesus Christ.

PHILIPPIANS 1:6

He that is slow to wrath is of great understanding:
but he that is hasty of spirit exalteth folly.
PROVERBS 14:29

What man is he that desireth life, and loveth many days,
that he may see good? Keep thy tongue from evil,
and thy lips from speaking guile.
PSALM 34:12–13

Let all bitterness, and wrath, and anger, and clamour, and
evil speaking, be put away from you, with all malice: and be
ye kind one to another, tenderhearted, forgiving one another,
even as God for Christ's sake hath forgiven you.
EPHESIANS 4:31–32

He that hath knowledge spareth his words: and a man
of understanding is of an excellent spirit. Even a fool,
when he holdeth his peace, is counted wise: and he that
shutteth his lips is esteemed a man of understanding.
PROVERBS 17:27–28

And the very God of peace sanctify you wholly; and I pray
God your whole spirit and soul and body be preserved
blameless unto the coming of our Lord Jesus Christ.
1 THESSALONIANS 5:23

He that is slow to anger is better than the mighty;
and he that ruleth his spirit than he that taketh a city.

PROVERBS 16:32

Create in me a clean heart, O God; and renew a right spirit
within me. Cast me not away from thy presence; and take
not thy holy spirit from me. Restore unto me the joy of
thy salvation; and uphold me with thy free spirit.

PSALM 51:10–12

A good man out of the good treasure of his heart bringeth
forth that which is good; and an evil man out of the evil
treasure of his heart bringeth forth that which is evil:
for of the abundance of the heart his mouth speaketh.

LUKE 6:45

For we ourselves also were sometimes foolish, disobedient,
deceived, serving divers lusts and pleasures, living in malice
and envy, hateful, and hating one another. But after that
the kindness and love of God our Saviour toward man
appeared, not by works of righteousness which we have
done, but according to his mercy he saved us, by the washing
of regeneration, and renewing of the Holy Ghost; which he
shed on us abundantly through Jesus Christ our Saviour.

TITUS 3:3–6

ANXIETY

Anxiety can show up in our bodies in many ways, from sweaty palms to full-blown panic attacks. Whatever its cause—fear, stress, bodily imbalances—we aren't at the mercy of our anxiety. Jesus is near to us in our distress, and in His Word He promises that He knows what we need from Him before we even ask. We can learn to recognize the situations and thoughts that trigger our anxiety or fear and practice bringing those things before our strong Protector. These Bible promises affirm that when we call to Him, He answers our cries with power and peace.

Be still, and know that I am God.
PSALM 46:10

Be careful for nothing; but in every thing by prayer and supplication with thanksgiving let your requests be made known unto God. And the peace of God, which passeth all understanding, shall keep your hearts and minds through Christ Jesus.
PHILIPPIANS 4:6–7

*Blessed is the man that trusteth in the L*ORD*, and whose*
*hope the L*ORD *is. For he shall be as a tree planted by the*
waters, and that spreadeth out her roots by the river,
and shall not see when heat cometh, but her leaf shall be
green; and shall not be careful in the year of drought,
neither shall cease from yielding fruit.

JEREMIAH 17:7–8

Are not two sparrows sold for a farthing? and one of
them shall not fall on the ground without your Father.
But the very hairs of your head are all numbered.
Fear ye not therefore, ye are of more
value than many sparrows.

MATTHEW 10:29–31

He that dwelleth in the secret place of the most High
shall abide under the shadow of the Almighty.
*I will say of the L*ORD*, He is my refuge and*
my fortress: my God; in him will I trust.

PSALM 91:1–2

The Lord is on my side; I will not fear:
what can man do unto me?

PSALM 118:6

*But now thus saith the LORD that created thee, O Jacob,
and he that formed thee, O Israel, fear not: for I have
redeemed thee, I have called thee by thy name; thou art
mine. When thou passest through the waters, I will be
with thee; and through the rivers, they shall not overflow
thee: when thou walkest through the fire, thou shalt not be
burned; neither shall the flame kindle upon thee.*

ISAIAH 43:1–2

Casting all your care upon him; for he careth for you.

1 PETER 5:7

*Behold, God is my salvation; I will trust, and not
be afraid: for the LORD JEHOVAH is my strength
and my song; he also is become my salvation.*

ISAIAH 12:2

*Who shall separate us from the love of Christ? shall
tribulation, or distress, or persecution, or famine, or
nakedness, or peril, or sword? As it is written, for thy sake
we are killed all the day long; we are accounted as sheep
for the slaughter. Nay, in all these things we are more
than conquerors through him that loved us.*

ROMANS 8:35–37

LORD, my heart is not haughty, nor mine eyes lofty:
neither do I exercise myself in great matters, or in things
too high for me. Surely I have behaved and quieted
myself, as a child that is weaned of his mother:
my soul is even as a weaned child.

PSALM 131:1–2

But Zion said, The LORD hath forsaken me, and my
Lord hath forgotten me. Can a woman forget her sucking
child, that she should not have compassion on the son of
her womb? yea, they may forget, yet will I not forget thee.
Behold, I have graven thee upon the palms of my
hands; thy walls are continually before me.

ISAIAH 49:14–16

For I the LORD thy God will hold thy right hand,
saying unto thee, Fear not; I will help thee.

ISAIAH 41:13

He shall cover thee with his feathers, and under his wings
shalt thou trust: his truth shall be thy shield and buckler.
Thou shalt not be afraid for the terror by night; nor for the
arrow that flieth by day; nor for the pestilence that walketh
in darkness; nor for the destruction that wasteth at noonday.

PSALM 91:4–6

BLESSINGS

When we're waiting for God to answer the prayers closest to our hearts, we can lose sight of how He shows us love through His daily blessings. He sends us friends who pray for us, the beauty of creation, and faithful reminders in His Word of how we can never be taken out of His hands. It can be hard, but look around you. Find the people and activities that continually breathe life and joy into you in the midst of this difficult time. Meditate on these Bible promises that show how God gives good gifts to His children!

Blessed be the God and Father of our Lord Jesus Christ,
who hath blessed us with all spiritual blessings
in heavenly places in Christ.

Ephesians 1:3

For the earth which drinketh in the rain that cometh
oft upon it, and bringeth forth herbs meet for them by
whom it is dressed, receiveth blessing from God.

Hebrews 6:7

My soul shall be satisfied as with marrow and
fatness; and my mouth shall praise thee with
joyful lips: when I remember thee upon my bed,
and meditate on thee in the night watches.

PSALM 63:5–6

And God is able to make all grace abound toward you;
that ye, always having all sufficiency in all things, may
abound to every good work: (As it is written, He hath
dispersed abroad; he hath given to the poor: his righteousness
remaineth for ever. Now he that ministereth seed to the
sower both minister bread for your food, and multiply your
seed sown, and increase the fruits of your righteousness;)
Being enriched in every thing to all bountifulness,
which causeth through us thanksgiving to God.

2 CORINTHIANS 9:8–11

Every good gift and every perfect gift is from above,
and cometh down from the Father of lights, with whom
is no variableness, neither shadow of turning.

JAMES 1:17

For the LORD God is a sun and shield: the LORD
will give grace and glory: no good thing will he
withhold from them that walk uprightly.

PSALM 84:11

I will be as the dew unto Israel: he shall grow as the lily, and cast forth his roots as Lebanon. His branches shall spread, and his beauty shall be as the olive tree, and his smell as Lebanon. They that dwell under his shadow shall return; they shall revive as the corn, and grow as the vine: the scent thereof shall be as the wine of Lebanon. Ephraim shall say, What have I to do any more with idols? I have heard him, and observed him: I am like a green fir tree. From me is thy fruit found.

HOSEA 14:5–8

Then was our mouth filled with laughter, and our tongue with singing: then said they among the heathen, The LORD hath done great things for them.

PSALM 126:2

And I will make them and the places round about my hill a blessing; and I will cause the shower to come down in his season; there shall be showers of blessing. And the tree of the field shall yield her fruit, and the earth shall yield her increase, and they shall be safe in their land, and shall know that I am the Lord, when I have broken the bands of their yoke, and delivered them out of the hand of those that served themselves of them.

EZEKIEL 34:26–27

Thus saith the LORD *that made thee, and formed thee from the womb, which will help thee; Fear not, O Jacob, my servant; and thou, Jesurun, whom I have chosen. For I will pour water upon him that is thirsty, and floods upon the dry ground: I will pour my spirit upon thy seed, and my blessing upon thine offspring: and they shall spring up as among the grass, as willows by the water courses.*

ISAIAH 44:2–4

Blessed be the Lord, who daily loadeth us with benefits, even the God of our salvation. Selah.

PSALM 68:19

I am come that they might have life, and that they might have it more abundantly.

JOHN 10:10

BROKEN-HEARTED

Our emotions and our bodies are inextricably connected. Just as chronic pain can cause depression, heartbreak can initiate a downward spiral in our physical health. What has broken your heart? Sometimes the fallen world cracks us open, or others clumsily handle us when we're at our most vulnerable. We might ache, realizing how far we still have to go before we're healed. When we find ourselves in pieces, God is gentle with our shards; He is the skillful mender of broken hearts. Read these Bible promises, and be assured that your compassionate Creator loves you deeply, pieces and all.

That Christ may dwell in your hearts by faith;
that ye, being rooted and grounded in love, may be able to
comprehend with all saints what is the breadth, and length,
and depth, and height; and to know the love of Christ,
which passeth knowledge, that ye might be filled
with all the fulness of God.

EPHESIANS 3:17–19

*The LORD is nigh unto them that are of a broken
heart; and saveth such as be of a contrite spirit.*

PSALM 34:18

*The Spirit of the Lord GOD is upon me; because the LORD
hath anointed me to preach good tidings unto the meek;
he hath sent me to bind up the brokenhearted, to proclaim
liberty to the captives, and the opening of the prison to them
that are bound; to proclaim the acceptable year of the LORD,
and the day of vengeance of our God; to comfort all that
mourn; to appoint unto them that mourn in Zion, to give
unto them beauty for ashes, the oil of joy for mourning,
the garment of praise for the spirit of heaviness; that they
might be called trees of righteousness, the planting
of the LORD, that he might be glorified.*

ISAIAH 61:1–3

*He healeth the broken in heart,
and bindeth up their wounds.*

PSALM 147:3

*The spirit of a man will sustain his infirmity;
but a wounded spirit who can bear?*

PROVERBS 18:14

*And we have known and believed the love that
God hath to us. God is love; and he that dwelleth
in love dwelleth in God, and God in him.*

1 JOHN 4:16

*The Lord upholdeth all that fall, and raiseth
up all those that be bowed down.*

PSALM 145:14

*My flesh and my heart faileth: but God is
the strength of my heart, and my portion for ever.*

PSALM 73:26

*Trust in the LORD with all thine heart; and lean
not unto thine own understanding. In all thy ways
acknowledge him, and he shall direct thy paths.*

PROVERBS 3:5–6

*O LORD, thou hast searched me, and known me. Thou
knowest my downsitting and mine uprising, thou
understandest my thought afar off. Thou compassest my
path and my lying down, and art acquainted with
all my ways. For there is not a word in my tongue,
but, lo, O LORD, thou knowest it altogether.*

PSALM 139:1–4

Blessed are the poor in spirit: for theirs is the kingdom of heaven. Blessed are they that mourn: for they shall be comforted.

MATTHEW 5:3–4

But do thou for me, O GOD the Lord, for thy name's sake: because thy mercy is good, deliver thou me. For I am poor and needy, and my heart is wounded within me.

PSALM 109:21–22

Thou tellest my wanderings: put thou my tears into thy bottle: are they not in thy book? In God will I praise his word: in the LORD will I praise his word.

PSALM 56:8, 10

I will turn their mourning into joy, and will comfort them, and make them rejoice from their sorrow.

JEREMIAH 31:13

And I will restore to you the years that the locust hath eaten, the cankerworm, and the caterpiller, and the palmerworm, my great army which I sent among you. And ye shall eat in plenty, and be satisfied, and praise the name of the LORD your God, that hath dealt wondrously with you: and my people shall never be ashamed.

JOEL 2:25–26

COMFORT

God isn't offended by our weeping or mourning—His heart is compassionate toward His children when they need comfort for their pain. Jesus gave us the Holy Spirit to be our Comforter. The Spirit prays for us when we have no words to speak for ourselves, and He guides us to the truth in the Word that we need at that moment. He can bring peace to our hearts through prayer and reading the Word even when the circumstances in our lives haven't changed yet. Read these Bible promises, and know that God never ignores our pleas for comfort.

Yea, though I walk through the valley of the shadow of death, I will fear no evil: for thou art with me; thy rod and thy staff they comfort me.
PSALM 23:4

Sing, O heavens; and be joyful, O earth; and break forth into singing, O mountains: for the LORD hath comforted his people, and will have mercy upon his afflicted.
ISAIAH 49:13

*Now our Lord Jesus Christ himself, and God, even our
Father, which hath loved us, and hath given us everlasting
consolation and good hope through grace, comfort your
hearts, and stablish you in every good word and work.*

2 THESSALONIANS 2:16–17

*Blessed be God, even the Father of our Lord Jesus
Christ, the Father of mercies, and the God of all comfort;
who comforteth us in all our tribulation, that we may
be able to comfort them which are in any trouble, by the
comfort wherewith we ourselves are comforted of God.
For as the sufferings of Christ abound in us, so our
consolation also aboundeth by Christ.*

2 CORINTHIANS 1:3–5

*But now thus saith the Lord that created thee, O Jacob,
and he that formed thee, O Israel, Fear not: for I have
redeemed thee, I have called thee by thy name; thou art
mine. When thou passest through the waters, I will be
with thee; and through the rivers, they shall not overflow
thee: when thou walkest through the fire, thou shalt not
be burned; neither shall the flame kindle upon thee.*

ISAIAH 43:1–2

Likewise the Spirit also helpeth our infirmities: for we know not what we should pray for as we ought: but the Spirit itself maketh intercession for us with groanings which cannot be uttered. And he that searcheth the hearts knoweth what is the mind of the Spirit, because he maketh intercession for the saints according to the will of God.

Romans 8:26–27

For thou hast delivered my soul from death: wilt not thou deliver my feet from falling, that I may walk before God in the light of the living?

Psalm 56:13

Thou wilt keep him in perfect peace, whose mind is stayed on thee: because he trusteth in thee.

Isaiah 26:3

Thou hast turned for me my mourning into dancing: thou hast put off my sackcloth, and girded me with gladness.

Psalm 30:11

Are not two sparrows sold for a farthing? and one of them shall not fall on the ground without your Father. But the very hairs of your head are all numbered. Fear ye not therefore, ye are of more value than many sparrows.

Matthew 10:29–31

And he lifted up his eyes on his disciples, and said,
Blessed be ye poor: for yours is the kingdom of God.
Blessed are ye that hunger now: for ye shall be filled.
Blessed are ye that weep now: for ye shall laugh.

LUKE 6:20–21

I will lift up mine eyes unto the hills, from whence cometh
my help. My help cometh from the LORD, which made
heaven and earth. He will not suffer thy foot to be moved:
he that keepeth thee will not slumber. Behold, he that
keepeth Israel shall neither slumber nor sleep. The LORD is
thy keeper: the LORD is thy shade upon thy right hand.

PSALM 121:1–5

COMMUNITY

When God created Eve, He demonstrated the necessity of community—"It is not good that the man should be alone" (Genesis 2:18). On our healing journey, we too need the loving support of a community. Not everyone will be a good fit, but God will provide those careful listeners, encouragers, and helpers we need to strengthen us. Whether we realize it or not, our community needs us too! We are a vital part of its life. Dwell on these Bible promises about the holy beauty of Christian fellowship—if you need a community, ask your heavenly Father, and He will provide.

Fulfil ye my joy, that ye be likeminded, having the same love, being of one accord, of one mind. Let nothing be done through strife or vainglory; but in lowliness of mind let each esteem other better than themselves. Look not every man on his own things, but every man also on the things of others. Let this mind be in you, which was also in Christ Jesus.

PHILIPPIANS 2:2–5

Two are better than one; because they have a good reward
for their labour. For if they fall, the one will lift up his
fellow: but woe to him that is alone when he falleth; for he
hath not another to help him up. Again, if two lie together,
then they have heat: but how can one be warm alone?
And if one prevail against him, two shall withstand
him; and a threefold cord is not quickly broken.
ECCLESIASTES 4:9–12

Behold, how good and how pleasant it is for brethren to
dwell together in unity! It is like the precious ointment upon
the head, that ran down upon the beard, even Aaron's
beard: that went down to the skirts of his garments.
PSALM 133:1–2

Bear ye one another's burdens,
and so fulfil the law of Christ.
GALATIANS 6:2

But speaking the truth in love, [we] may grow up into him
in all things, which is the head, even Christ: from whom
the whole body fitly joined together and compacted by
that which every joint supplieth, according to the effectual
working in the measure of every part, maketh increase
of the body unto the edifying of itself in love.
EPHESIANS 4:15–16

*This is my commandment, that ye love one another,
as I have loved you. Greater love hath no man than
this, that a man lay down his life for his friends.*
JOHN 15:12–13

*Let love be without dissimulation. Abhor that which is
evil; cleave to that which is good. Be kindly affectioned
one to another with brotherly love; in honour preferring
one another; not slothful in business; fervent in spirit;
serving the Lord; rejoicing in hope; patient in tribulation;
continuing instant in prayer; distributing to the
necessity of saints; given to hospitality.*
ROMANS 12:9–13

*Confess your faults one to another, and pray one for
another, that ye may be healed. The effectual fervent
prayer of a righteous man availeth much.*
JAMES 5:16

*A friend loveth at all times,
and a brother is born for adversity.*
PROVERBS 17:17

*And above all things have fervent charity among
yourselves: for charity shall cover the multitude of sins.
Use hospitality one to another without grudging.*
1 PETER 4:8–9

Neither pray I for these alone, but for them also which shall believe on me through their word; that they all may be one; as thou, Father, art in me, and I in thee, that they also may be one in us: that the world may believe that thou hast sent me. And the glory which thou gavest me I have given them; that they may be one, even as we are one: I in them, and thou in me, that they may be made perfect in one; and that the world may know that thou hast sent me, and hast loved them, as thou hast loved me.

JOHN 17:20–23

That there should be no schism in the body; but that the members should have the same care one for another. And whether one member suffer, all the members suffer with it; or one member be honoured, all the members rejoice with it. Now ye are the body of Christ, and members in particular.

1 CORINTHIANS 12:25–27

COURAGE

Courage doesn't mean that you are fearless. Instead, having courage means choosing to face the challenges before you and entrusting yourself—your fears and your efforts—to God. Maybe today's hurdle is getting out of bed for the first time in two days. Maybe it's finally making that phone call to ask for forgiveness. Perhaps it's yet another visit to the doctor that you've been dreading. Through everything, pray and ask to feel your Savior's presence go with you. Meditate on these Bible promises that proclaim that God's presence and strength can embolden us even in our most fearful moments.

Fear thou not; for I am with thee: be not dismayed; for I am thy God: I will strengthen thee; yea, I will help thee; yea, I will uphold thee with the right hand of my righteousness.
ISAIAH 41:10

Finally, my brethren, be strong in the Lord, and in the power of his might.
EPHESIANS 6:10

Have not I commanded thee? Be strong and of a good courage; be not afraid, neither be thou dismayed: for the LORD thy God is with thee whithersoever thou goest.

Joshua 1:9

Be strong and of a good courage, fear not, nor be afraid of them: for the LORD thy God, he it is that doth go with thee; he will not fail thee, nor forsake thee.

Deuteronomy 31:6

For God hath not given us the spirit of fear; but of power, and of love, and of a sound mind.

2 Timothy 1:7

These things I have spoken unto you, that in me ye might have peace. In the world ye shall have tribulation: but be of good cheer; I have overcome the world.

John 16:33

Be of good courage, and he shall strengthen your heart, all ye that hope in the Lord.

Psalm 31:24

For he hath said, I will never leave thee, nor forsake thee. So that we may boldly say, The Lord is my helper, and I will not fear what man shall do unto me.

Hebrews 13:5–6

But we have this treasure in earthen vessels, that the excellency of the power may be of God, and not of us. We are troubled on every side, yet not distressed; we are perplexed, but not in despair; persecuted, but not forsaken; cast down, but not destroyed; always bearing about in the body the dying of the Lord Jesus, that the life also of Jesus might be made manifest in our body. For we which live are always delivered unto death for Jesus' sake, that the life also of Jesus might be made manifest in our mortal flesh.

2 CORINTHIANS 4:7–11

In the fear of the LORD is strong confidence: and his children shall have a place of refuge.

PROVERBS 14:26

He that dwelleth in the secret place of the most High shall abide under the shadow of the Almighty. I will say of the Lord, He is my refuge and my fortress: my God; in him will I trust. He shall cover thee with his feathers, and under his wings shalt thou trust: his truth shall be thy shield and buckler. Thou shalt not be afraid for the terror by night; nor for the arrow that flieth by day; nor for the pestilence that walketh in darkness; nor for the destruction that wasteth at noonday.

PSALM 91:1–2, 4–6

The wicked flee when no man pursueth:
but the righteous are bold as a lion.

For thou wilt light my candle: the LORD my God will
enlighten my darkness. For by thee I have run through a
troop; and by my God have I leaped over a wall. As for
God, his way is perfect: the word of the LORD is tried:
he is a buckler to all those that trust in him. For who
is God save the LORD? or who is a rock save our God?

PSALM 18:28–31

Be strong and of good courage, and do it: fear not, nor be
dismayed: for the LORD God, even my God, will be with
thee; he will not fail thee, nor forsake thee.

1 CHRONICLES 28:20

DEPENDING ON GOD

Though certainty in life is an illusion, we love it all the same—and we miss it terribly when we're hit with the unexpected. There are no certainties in illness and recovery, just plans, probabilities, and "best results." God is our Rock and our Strong Deliverer during uncertainty. Though He doesn't always reveal what's coming next for us, we know He is unchangeable in His love, wisdom, and strength to help. In these Bible promises, the Word speaks with certainty that God blesses those who trust in His mercy, seek His wisdom, and draw their life from Him.

But let all those that put their trust in thee rejoice:
let them ever shout for joy, because thou defendest them:
let them also that love thy name be joyful in thee.

PSALM 5:11

The LORD upholdeth all that fall,
and raiseth up all those that be bowed down.

PSALM 145:14

It is better to trust in the LORD than to put
confidence in man. It is better to trust in the
LORD than to put confidence in princes.
PSALM 118:8–9

The LORD preserveth all them that love him.
PSALM 145:20

Because thou hast been my help, therefore in the shadow
of thy wings will I rejoice. My soul followeth hard
after thee: thy right hand upholdeth me.
PSALM 63:7–8

He that dwelleth in the secret place of the most High
shall abide under the shadow of the Almighty. I will
say of the LORD, He is my refuge and my fortress:
my God; in him will I trust. He shall cover thee with
his feathers, and under his wings shalt thou trust:
his truth shall be thy shield and buckler.
PSALM 91:1–2, 4

For the Lord loveth judgment, and forsaketh
not his saints; they are preserved for ever:
but the seed of the wicked shall be cut off.
PSALM 37:28

Seek the Lord, and his strength:
seek his face evermore.
PSALM 105:4

The fear of man bringeth a snare: but whoso
putteth his trust in the Lord shall be safe.
PROVERBS 29:25

Because he hath set his love upon me, therefore will
I deliver him: I will set him on high, because he hath
known my name. He shall call upon me, and I will
answer him: I will be with him in trouble; I will
deliver him, and honour him. With long life will
I satisfy him, and shew him my salvation.
PSALM 91:14–16

The Lord shall preserve thee from all evil: he shall preserve
thy soul. The Lord shall preserve thy going out and thy
coming in from this time forth, and even for evermore.
PSALM 121:7–8

And the Lord, he it is that doth go before thee;
he will be with thee, he will not fail thee,
neither forsake thee: fear not, neither be dismayed.
DEUTERONOMY 31:8

*For the Lord G*ᴏᴅ *will help me; therefore shall I not be confounded: therefore have I set my face like a flint, and I know that I shall not be ashamed.*

Iꜱᴀɪᴀʜ 50:7

*Trust in the L*ᴏʀᴅ *with all thine heart; and lean not unto thine own understanding. In all thy ways acknowledge him, and he shall direct thy paths.*

Pʀᴏᴠᴇʀʙꜱ 3:5–6

*Behold, as the eyes of servants look unto the hand of their masters, and as the eyes of a maiden unto the hand of her mistress; so our eyes wait upon the L*ᴏʀᴅ *our God, until that he have mercy upon us.*

Pꜱᴀʟᴍ 123:2

Lead me in thy truth, and teach me: for thou art the God of my salvation; on thee do I wait all the day.

Pꜱᴀʟᴍ 25:5

*Blessed is the man that trusteth in the L*ᴏʀᴅ*, and whose hope the L*ᴏʀᴅ *is. For he shall be as a tree planted by the waters, and that spreadeth out her roots by the river, and shall not see when heat cometh, but her leaf shall be green; and shall not be careful in the year of drought, neither shall cease from yielding fruit.*

Jᴇʀᴇᴍɪᴀʜ 17:7–8

DEPRESSION

Many faithful men and women in scripture dealt with the despondency and intense sadness of depression. They cried out to God, and He answered them in their emotional, physical, and spiritual need. Today, we are blessed with information about many kinds of depression, as well as health professionals and counselors whom God has gifted with the skills to help and heal. As you explore the options to best care for yourself, read these Bible promises and remember that God loves you beyond measure. He's near to you in your pain, and His gentle strength will guide and lift you up.

I waited patiently for the LORD; and he inclined unto me, and heard my cry. He brought me up also out of an horrible pit, out of the miry clay, and set my feet upon a rock, and established my goings. And he hath put a new song in my mouth, even praise unto our God: many shall see it, and fear, and shall trust in the LORD.

PSALM 40:1–3

Thou tellest my wanderings: put thou my tears into thy bottle:
are they not in thy book? In God will I praise his word: in the
LORD will I praise his word. In God have I put my trust:
I will not be afraid what man can do unto me.

PSALM 56:8, 10–11

Trust in him at all times; ye people, pour out your
heart before him: God is a refuge for us. Selah.

PSALM 62:8

And the LORD, he it is that doth go before thee;
he will be with thee, he will not fail thee,
neither forsake thee: fear not, neither be dismayed.

DEUTERONOMY 31:8

The LORD is nigh unto them that are of a broken
heart; and saveth such as be of a contrite spirit.
Many are the afflictions of the righteous:
but the LORD delivereth him out of them all.

PSALM 34:18–19

Why art thou cast down, O my soul? and why
art thou disquieted within me? hope thou in God:
for I shall yet praise him, who is the health
of my countenance, and my God.

PSALM 42:11

Through the tender mercy of our God; whereby the dayspring from on high hath visited us, to give light to them that sit in darkness and in the shadow of death, to guide our feet into the way of peace.

LUKE 1:78–79

Likewise the Spirit also helpeth our infirmities: for we know not what we should pray for as we ought: but the Spirit itself maketh intercession for us with groanings which cannot be uttered.

ROMANS 8:26

Humble yourselves therefore under the mighty hand of God, that he may exalt you in due time: casting all your care upon him; for he careth for you.

1 PETER 5:6–7

My heart is smitten, and withered like grass; so that I forget to eat my bread. By reason of the voice of my groaning my bones cleave to my skin. I watch, and am as a sparrow alone upon the house top. But thou, O Lord, shall endure for ever; and thy remembrance unto all generations. Thou shalt arise, and have mercy upon Zion: for the time to favour her, yea, the set time, is come.

PSALM 102:4–5, 7, 12–13

Not that I speak in respect of want: for I have learned,
in whatsoever state I am, therewith to be content.
I know both how to be abased, and I know how to abound:
every where and in all things I am instructed both to be
full and to be hungry, both to abound and to suffer need.
I can do all things through Christ which strengtheneth me.
PHILIPPIANS 4:11–13

Therefore I will look unto the LORD; I will wait for the God
of my salvation: my God will hear me. Rejoice not against
me, O mine enemy: when I fall, I shall arise; when I
sit in darkness, the LORD shall be a light unto me.
MICAH 7:7–8

ENCOURAGEMENT

During the healing process, we are especially vulnerable to worry and despair. When the light of hope in our hearts fades to a flicker, the Holy Spirit sends encouragement to fan the flame. He communicates God's truth and love to us through other believers, prayer, and our time in the Word. Sometimes He sends encouragement when we least expect it—a hilarious joke, or an empathetic stranger at the grocery store. We too can share the encouragement He's given us! Read these Bible promises about the power of encouragement—God can enliven your heart even on its most trying days.

That Christ may dwell in your hearts by faith;
that ye, being rooted and grounded in love, may be
able to comprehend with all saints what is the breadth,
and length, and depth, and height; and to know the
love of Christ, which passeth knowledge, that ye
might be filled with all the fulness of God.

EPHESIANS 3:17–19

The LORD is my strength and song, and is become
my salvation. The voice of rejoicing and salvation
is in the tabernacles of the righteous: the right
hand of the LORD doeth valiantly.

PSALM 118:14–15

For God hath not given us the spirit of fear;
a but of power, and of love, and of a sound mind.

2 TIMOTHY 1:7

God is our refuge and strength, a very present
help in trouble. Therefore will not we fear, though
the earth be removed, and though the mountains be
carried into the midst of the sea; though the waters
thereof roar and be troubled, though the mountains
shake with the swelling thereof. Selah.

PSALM 46:1–3

Now our Lord Jesus Christ himself, and God, even our
Father, which hath loved us, and hath given us everlasting
consolation and good hope through grace, comfort your
hearts, and stablish you in every good word and work.

2 THESSALONIANS 2:16–17

Heaviness in the heart of man maketh it stoop:
but a good word maketh it glad.

PROVERBS 12:25

But be filled with the Spirit; speaking to yourselves
in psalms and hymns and spiritual songs, singing
and making melody in your heart to the Lord;
giving thanks always for all things unto God and
the Father in the name of our Lord Jesus Christ.

EPHESIANS 5:18–20

For whatsoever things were written aforetime were
written for our learning, that we through patience
and comfort of the scriptures might have hope.

ROMANS 15:4

For whatsoever is born of God overcometh the world:
and this is the victory that overcometh the world,
even our faith. Who is he that overcometh the world,
but he that believeth that Jesus is the Son of God?

1 JOHN 5:4–5

The LORD thy God in the midst of thee is mighty;
he will save, he will rejoice over thee with joy; he will
rest in his love, he will joy over thee with singing.

ZEPHANIAH 3:17

Fear thou not; for I am with thee: be not dismayed; for I am
thy God: I will strengthen thee; yea, I will help thee; yea,
I will uphold thee with the right hand of my righteousness.
ISAIAH 41:10

And this is the confidence that we have in him, that,
if we ask any thing according to his will, he heareth us:
and if we know that he hear us, whatsoever we ask,
we know that we have the petitions that we desired of him.
1 JOHN 5:14–15

Now unto him that is able to do exceeding abundantly
above all that we ask or think, according to the power that
worketh in us, unto him be glory in the church by Christ
Jesus throughout all ages, world without end. Amen.
EPHESIANS 3:20–21

What shall we then say to these things?
If God be for us, who can be against us?
ROMANS 8:31

The LORD hath appeared of old unto me, saying,
Yea, I have loved thee with an everlasting love:
therefore with lovingkindness have I drawn thee.
JEREMIAH 31:3

ETERNITY

As God's people, we are pilgrims on this earth, serving faithfully as we look forward to our true home in heaven with Christ. The hope of eternity is even sweeter for those of us who suffer bodily now, because we know that no matter the severity of our condition, we will be completely healed in Jesus' presence. He has promised to make all things—and us—new! Hold on to these Bible promises when the present hurt grows too heavy to bear—eternity has no more tears or pain, and we will live forever in the light of our beautiful Savior.

Thou shalt guide me with thy counsel,
and afterward receive me to glory.
PSALM 73:24

Beloved, now are we the sons of God, and it doth not yet
appear what we shall be: but we know that, when he shall
appear, we shall be like him; for we shall see him as he is.
1 JOHN 3:2

And there shall be no more curse: but the throne of God and of the Lamb shall be in it; and his servants shall serve him: and they shall see his face; and his name shall be in their foreheads. And there shall be no night there; and they need no candle, neither light of the sun; for the Lord God giveth them light: and they shall reign for ever and ever.

REVELATION 22:3–5

For, behold, I create new heavens and a new earth: and the former shall not be remembered, nor come into mind. But be ye glad and rejoice for ever in that which I create: for, behold, I create Jerusalem a rejoicing, and her people a joy. And I will rejoice in Jerusalem, and joy in my people: and the voice of weeping shall be no more heard in her, nor the voice of crying.

ISAIAH 65:17–19

And I heard a great voice out of heaven saying, Behold, the tabernacle of God is with men, and he will dwell with them, and they shall be his people, and God himself shall be with them, and be their God. And God shall wipe away all tears from their eyes; and there shall be no more death, neither sorrow, nor crying, neither shall there be any more pain: for the former things are passed away.

REVELATION 21:3–4

*Therefore they shall come and sing in the height of Zion, and shall flow together to the goodness of the L*ORD*, for wheat, and for wine, and for oil, and for the young of the flock and of the herd: and their soul shall be as a watered garden; and they shall not sorrow any more at all. Then shall the virgin rejoice in the dance, both young men and old together: for I will turn their mourning into joy, and will comfort them, and make them rejoice from their sorrow.*

JEREMIAH 31:12–13

And I give unto them eternal life; and they shall never perish, neither shall any man pluck them out of my hand.

JOHN 10:28

And this is the Father's will which hath sent me, that of all which he hath given me I should lose nothing, but should raise it up again at the last day. And this is the will of him that sent me, that every one which seeth the Son, and believeth on him, may have everlasting life: and I will raise him up at the last day.

JOHN 6:39–40

Then shall the King say unto them on his right hand, Come, ye blessed of my Father, inherit the kingdom prepared for you from the foundation of the world.

MATTHEW 25:34

In my Father's house are many mansions: if it were not so, I would have told you. I go to prepare a place for you. And if I go and prepare a place for you, I will come again, and receive you unto myself; that where I am, there ye may be also.

JOHN 14:2–3

Then we which are alive and remain shall be caught up together with them in the clouds, to meet the Lord in the air: and so shall we ever be with the Lord.

1 THESSALONIANS 4:17

FAITH

Faith is being confident of God's promises even when we can't see when they'll be fulfilled. Maybe someone's told you, "If you had more faith, you'd be healed." God isn't waiting for us to "believe enough"; He wants us to put our faith in His power and His good plan for us, not in how much we believe. Just like the saints of old, we can trust our faithful God to sustain us without us knowing all the details. Read these Bible promises, and see how God strengthens our hearts to trust His good plan even during our hardest journeys.

Now faith is the substance of things hoped for,
the evidence of things not seen.

HEBREWS 11:1

Who is among you that feareth the LORD, that obeyeth
the voice of his servant, that walketh in darkness,
and hath no light? let him trust in the name
of the LORD, and stay upon his God.

ISAIAH 50:10

Jesus answered and said unto them, Verily I say unto you, if ye have faith, and doubt not, ye shall not only do this which is done to the fig tree, but also if ye shall say unto this mountain, Be thou removed, and be thou cast into the sea; it shall be done. And all things, whatsoever ye shall ask in prayer, believing, ye shall receive.

MATTHEW 21:21–22

But with the precious blood of Christ, as of a lamb without blemish and without spot: who by him do believe in God, that raised him up from the dead, and gave him glory; that your faith and hope might be in God.

1 PETER 1:19, 21

But without faith it is impossible to please him: for he that cometh to God must believe that he is, and that he is a rewarder of them that diligently seek him.

HEBREWS 11:6

For whatsoever is born of God overcometh the world: and this is the victory that overcometh the world, even our faith. Who is he that overcometh the world, but he that believeth that Jesus is the Son of God?

1 JOHN 5:4–5

For therein is the righteousness of God revealed from faith to faith: as it is written, the just shall live by faith.

ROMANS 1:17

I have fought a good fight, I have finished my course, I have kept the faith: henceforth there is laid up for me a crown of righteousness, which the Lord, the righteous judge, shall give me at that day: and not to me only, but unto all them also that love his appearing.

2 TIMOTHY 4:7–8

Cast not away therefore your confidence, which hath great recompence of reward. For ye have need of patience, that, after ye have done the will of God, ye might receive the promise.

HEBREWS 10:35–36

Say to them that are of a fearful heart, Be strong, fear not: behold, your God will come with vengeance, even God with a recompence; he will come and save you.

ISAIAH 35:4

Jesus cried and said, He that believeth on me, believeth not on me, but on him that sent me. And he that seeth me seeth him that sent me. I am come a light into the world, that whosoever believeth on me should not abide in darkness.

JOHN 12:44–46

These all died in faith, not having received the promises,
but having seen them afar off, and were persuaded of them,
and embraced them, and confessed that they were strangers
and pilgrims on the earth. For they that say such things
declare plainly that they seek a country. And truly, if they
had been mindful of that country from whence they came
out, they might have had opportunity to have returned.
But now they desire a better country, that is, an heavenly:
wherefore God is not ashamed to be called their God:
for he hath prepared for them a city.

HEBREWS 11:13–16

This is the confidence that we have in him, that,
if we ask anything according to his will, he heareth us.

1 JOHN 5:14

FORGIVENESS

As we walk through life, God's forgiveness is a precious assurance. We can stand boldly in His presence, knowing that Jesus has already paid for our every sin and shame. Because He has so generously covered our sins with love, God calls us to reflect Him by forgiving those who have wronged us. Depending on the offense, we may have to bring our hurt to the Father again and again, asking for His strength and compassion to forgive. These Bible promises show that we can be confident in God's forgiveness and that He will help us extend forgiveness to others.

Who is a God like unto thee, that pardoneth iniquity, and passeth by the transgression of the remnant of his heritage? he retaineth not his anger for ever, because he delighteth in mercy. He will turn again, he will have compassion upon us; he will subdue our iniquities; and thou wilt cast all their sins into the depths of the sea.
MICAH 7:18–19

I have blotted out, as a thick cloud, thy transgressions,
and, as a cloud, thy sins: return unto me;
for I have redeemed thee.

ISAIAH 44:22

And you, being dead in your sins and the uncircumcision
of your flesh, hath he quickened together with him, having
forgiven you all trespasses; blotting out the handwriting of
ordinances that was against us, which was contrary to us,
and took it out of the way, nailing it to his cross.

COLOSSIANS 2:13–14

He hath not dealt with us after our sins; nor rewarded
us according to our iniquities. For as the heaven is high
above the earth, so great is his mercy toward them that
fear him. As far as the east is from the west, so far
hath he removed our transgressions from us.

PSALM 103:10–12

Whereof the Holy Ghost also is a witness to us: for after that
he had said before, this is the covenant that I will make
with them after those days, saith the Lord, I will put my
laws into their hearts, and in their minds will I write them;
and their sins and iniquities will I remember no more. Now
where remission of these is, there is no more offering for sin.

HEBREWS 10:15–18

*If we confess our sins, he is faithful and just to forgive us
our sins, and to cleanse us from all unrighteousness.*
1 JOHN 1:9

*Blessed is he whose transgression is forgiven, whose sin is
covered. Blessed is the man unto whom the LORD imputeth
not iniquity, and in whose spirit there is no guile.*
PSALM 32:1–2

*For if ye forgive men their trespasses, your heavenly Father
will also forgive you: but if ye forgive not men their
trespasses, neither will your Father forgive your trespasses.*
MATTHEW 6:14–15

*Forbearing one another, and forgiving one another,
if any man have a quarrel against any:
even as Christ forgave you, so also do ye.*
COLOSSIANS 3:13

*Let all bitterness, and wrath, and anger, and clamour, and
evil speaking, be put away from you, with all malice: and be
ye kind one to another, tenderhearted, forgiving one another,
even as God for Christ's sake hath forgiven you.*
EPHESIANS 4:31–32

*He that covereth a transgression seeketh love; but he
that repeateth a matter separateth very friends.*
PROVERBS 17:9

*Finally, be ye all of one mind, having compassion one
of another, love as brethren, be pitiful, be courteous:
not rendering evil for evil, or railing for railing: but
contrariwise blessing; knowing that ye are thereunto
called, that ye should inherit a blessing.*
1 PETER 3:8–9

*And when ye stand praying, forgive, if ye have ought
against any: that your Father also which is in
heaven may forgive you your trespasses.*
MARK 11:25

*Follow peace with all men, and holiness, without which no
man shall see the Lord: looking diligently lest any man fail
of the grace of God; lest any root of bitterness springing
up trouble you, and thereby many be defiled.*
HEBREWS 12:14–15

FRUSTRATION

"Are You listening, God? I just can't handle this anymore!" We can get so frustrated with where we are physically or spiritually. It doesn't help matters when we deal with uncompassionate doctors, patronizing family members, or difficult side effects of medication. Many heroes of the Bible also felt this bone-deep frustration. Yet in the midst of venting their pain and fear to God, they also held on to their belief in His goodness. Read these groups of verses that show examples of God's people crying out to Him in frustration and how their hearts found comfort in His powerful promises.

Have mercy upon me, O LORD; for I am weak: O LORD, heal me; for my bones are vexed. My soul is also sore vexed: but thou, O LORD, how long? Depart from me, all ye workers of iniquity; for the LORD hath heard the voice of my weeping. The LORD hath heard my supplication; the LORD will receive my prayer.

PSALM 6:2–3, 8–9

69

My God, my God, why hast thou forsaken me? why art thou
so far from helping me, and from the words of my roaring?
O my God, I cry in the day time, but thou hearest not;
and in the night season, and am not silent. Ye that fear the
LORD, *praise him. . . . For he hath not despised nor abhorred*
the affliction of the afflicted; neither hath he hid his face
from him; but when he cried unto him, he heard.

PSALM 22:1–2, 23–24

Why is my pain perpetual, and my wound incurable, which
refuseth to be healed? wilt thou be altogether unto me as a
liar, and as waters that fail? And they shall fight against
thee, but they shall not prevail against thee: for I am with
thee to save thee and to deliver thee, saith the LORD.
And I will deliver thee out of the hand of the wicked,
and I will redeem thee out of the hand of the terrible.

JEREMIAH 15:18, 20–21

I am feeble and sore broken: I have roared by reason
of the disquietness of my heart. Lord, all my desire is
before thee; and my groaning is not hid from thee.
My heart panteth, my strength faileth me: as for the
light of mine eyes, it also is gone from me. For in thee,
O LORD, *do I hope: thou wilt hear, O Lord my God.*

PSALM 38:8–10, 15

And I said, My strength and my hope is perished from the LORD: remembering mine affliction and my misery, the wormwood and the gall. My soul hath them still in remembrance, and is humbled in me. This I recall to my mind, therefore have I hope. It is of the LORD's mercies that we are not consumed, because his compassions fail not. They are new every morning: great is thy faithfulness. The LORD is my portion, saith my soul; therefore will I hope in him.

LAMENTATIONS 3:18–24

Hath God forgotten to be gracious? hath he in anger shut up his tender mercies? Selah. And I said, This is my infirmity: but I will remember the years of the right hand of the most High. I will remember the works of the LORD: surely I will remember thy wonders of old.

PSALM 77:9–11

Thine hands have made me and fashioned me together round about; yet thou dost destroy me. Remember, I beseech thee, that thou hast made me as the clay; and wilt thou bring me into dust again? Thou hast clothed me with skin and flesh, and hast fenced me with bones and sinews. Thou hast granted me life and favour, and thy visitation hath preserved my spirit.

JOB 10:8–9, 11–12

I will say unto God my rock, Why hast thou forgotten me?
why go I mourning because of the oppression of the enemy?
As with a sword in my bones, mine enemies reproach me;
while they say daily unto me, Where is thy God? Why art
thou cast down, O my soul? and why art thou disquieted
within me? hope thou in God: for I shall yet praise him,
who is the health of my countenance, and my God.

PSALM 42:9–11

Therefore is my spirit overwhelmed within me;
my heart within me is desolate. I remember the days of
old; I meditate on all thy works; I muse on the work
of thy hands. I stretch forth my hands unto thee: my
soul thirsteth after thee, as a thirsty land. Selah.

PSALM 143:4–6

GOD IS IN CONTROL

Our heavenly Father is the sovereign King over all creation, so nothing can happen outside of His will. He sometimes allows difficult things to enter our lives, and though we wrestle with them, we know that nothing happens to us "on accident." God has a purpose for everything, and He works out everything for good to those who love Him. The Holy Spirit comforts and guides our hearts, helping us to continue trusting in God's loving sovereignty. Take courage from these Bible promises that attest that He reigns over all, down to the smallest details of our lives.

And we know that all things work together for
good to them that love God, to them who
are the called according to his purpose.
ROMANS 8:28

The LORD shall preserve thee from all evil: he shall preserve
thy soul. The LORD shall preserve thy going out and thy
coming in from this time forth, and even for evermore.
PSALM 121:7–8

Thine, O Lord is the greatness, and the power, and the glory, and the victory, and the majesty: for all that is in the heaven and in the earth is thine; thine is the kingdom, O Lord, and thou art exalted as head above all. Both riches and honour come of thee, and thou reignest over all; and in thine hand is power and might; and in thine hand it is to make great, and to give strength unto all.

1 Chronicles 29:11–12

And as Jesus passed by, he saw a man which was blind from his birth. And his disciples asked him, saying, Master, who did sin, this man, or his parents, that he was born blind? Jesus answered, Neither hath this man sinned, nor his parents: but that the works of God should be made manifest in him. When he had thus spoken, he spat on the ground, and made clay of the spittle, and he anointed the eyes of the blind man with the clay, and said unto him, Go, wash in the pool of Siloam, (which is by interpretation, Sent.) He went his way therefore, and washed, and came seeing.

John 9:1–3, 6–7

A man's heart deviseth his way: but the Lord directeth his steps.

Proverbs 16:9

Remember the former things of old: for I am God, and there is none else; I am God, and there is none like me, declaring the end from the beginning, and from ancient times the things that are not yet done, saying, My counsel shall stand, and I will do all my pleasure.

ISAIAH 46:9–10

For as the rain cometh down, and the snow from heaven, and returneth not thither, but watereth the earth, and maketh it bring forth and bud, that it may give seed to the sower, and bread to the eater: so shall my word be that goeth forth out of my mouth: it shall not return unto me void, but it shall accomplish that which I please, and it shall prosper in the thing whereto I sent it.

ISAIAH 55:10–11

And all the inhabitants of the earth are reputed as nothing: and he doeth according to his will in the army of heaven, and among the inhabitants of the earth: and none can stay his hand, or say unto him, What doest thou?

DANIEL 4:35

But Jesus beheld them, and said unto them, With men this is impossible; but with God all things are possible.

MATTHEW 19:26

The LORD killeth, and maketh alive: he bringeth down to the grave, and bringeth up. The LORD maketh poor, and maketh rich: he bringeth low, and lifteth up. He raiseth up the poor out of the dust, and lifteth up the beggar from the dunghill, to set them among princes, and to make them inherit the throne of glory: for the pillars of the earth are the LORD's, and he hath set the world upon them.

1 SAMUEL 2:6–8

For the word of the LORD is right; and all his works are done in truth.

PSALM 33:4

And all the trees of the field shall know that I the LORD have brought down the high tree, have exalted the low tree, have dried up the green tree, and have made the dry tree to flourish: I the LORD have spoken and have done it.

EZEKIEL 17:24

GOD'S GOODNESS

When we see or experience suffering, it's not unusual for us to question our Creator. "Aren't You good? Then why is this happening?" We must turn to the truth of the Word to realign our heart's vision. We daily experience the effects of a world mired in sin, and scripture testifies that God's people will suffer hardship in this life too. However, the Word also proclaims that God shows His eternal goodness, mercy, and strength toward all He loves! Meditate on these Bible promises that reveal His character, and reflect on how His goodness is present in your life.

He loveth righteousness and judgment:
the earth is full of the goodness of the LORD.
PSALM 33:5

Every good gift and every perfect gift is from above,
and cometh down from the Father of lights, with
whom is no variableness, neither shadow of turning.
JAMES 1:17

The LORD is good, a strong hold in the day of trouble;
and he knoweth them that trust in him.

NAHUM 1:7

Oh that men would praise the Lord for his goodness,
and for his wonderful works to the children of men!
For he satisfieth the longing soul, and filleth
the hungry soul with goodness.

PSALM 107:8–9

Oh how great is thy goodness, which thou hast laid up
for them that fear thee; which thou hast wrought for
them that trust in thee before the sons of men!

PSALM 31:19

I will mention the lovingkindnesses of the LORD,
and the praises of the LORD, according to all that the
LORD hath bestowed on us, and the great goodness
toward the house of Israel, which he hath bestowed
on them according to his mercies, and according to
the multitude of his lovingkindnesses.

ISAIAH 63:7

The blessing of the LORD, it maketh rich,
and he addeth no sorrow with it.

PROVERBS 10:22

As newborn babes, desire the sincere milk of
the word, that ye may grow thereby: if so be
ye have tasted that the Lord is gracious.
1 PETER 2:2–3

They shall abundantly utter the memory of thy great
goodness, and shall sing of thy righteousness. The Lord is
good to all: and his tender mercies are over all his works.
PSALM 145:7, 9

The earth, O LORD, is full of thy mercy: teach me thy
statutes. Thou hast dealt well with thy servant, O LORD,
according unto thy word. Teach me good judgment and
knowledge: for I have believed thy commandments. Before I
was afflicted I went astray: but now have I kept thy word.
Thou art good, and doest good; teach me thy statutes.
PSALM 119:64–68

But let him that glorieth glory in this, that he understandeth
and knoweth me, that I am the Lord which exercise
lovingkindness, judgment, and righteousness, in the earth:
for in these things I delight, saith the Lord.
JEREMIAH 9:24

For thou, Lord, art good, and ready to forgive;
and plenteous in mercy unto all them that call upon thee.
PSALM 86:5

If ye then, being evil, know how to give good gifts unto
your children, how much more shall your Father which
is in heaven give good things to them that ask him?
MATTHEW 7:11

Oh how great is thy goodness, which thou hast laid up
for them that fear thee; which thou hast wrought for
them that trust in thee before the sons of men!
PSALM 31:19

Remember not the sins of my youth, nor my transgressions:
according to thy mercy remember thou me for thy
goodness' sake, O LORD. Good and upright is the LORD:
therefore will he teach sinners in the way.
PSALM 25:7–8

Surely goodness and mercy shall follow me
all the days of my life: and I will dwell
in the house of the LORD for ever.
PSALM 23:6

GOD'S LOVE

It is so important to remember how much our Creator loves us, because it can be so hard for us to be kind to ourselves when we're hurting. We see our flaws, our shameful secrets, our failures. But God didn't lavish His love on us because we'd earned it. When we had no interest in loving Him, He demonstrated His love by sending Jesus to save us. God's powerful love animates our souls from death to abundant life in Christ. He loves you now and always will, no matter what. Soak up these Bible promises that demonstrate His unchanging love!

For God so loved the world, that he gave his only begotten Son, that whosoever believeth in him should not perish, but have everlasting life.

JOHN 3:16

The LORD hath appeared of old unto me, saying, Yea, I have loved thee with an everlasting love: therefore with lovingkindness have I drawn thee.

JEREMIAH 31:3

As the Father hath loved me, so have I loved you:
continue ye in my love. If ye keep my commandments,
ye shall abide in my love; even as I have kept my
Father's commandments, and abide in his love.
These things have I spoken unto you, that my joy
might remain in you, and that your joy might be full.
JOHN 15:9–11

For the mountains shall depart, and the hills be
removed; but my kindness shall not depart from thee,
neither shall the covenant of my peace be removed,
saith the LORD that hath mercy on thee.
ISAIAH 54:10

The LORD thy God in the midst of thee is mighty;
he will save, he will rejoice over thee with joy; he will
rest in his love, he will joy over thee with singing.
ZEPHANIAH 3:17

In this was manifested the love of God toward us,
because that God sent his only begotten Son into the
world, that we might live through him. Herein is love,
not that we loved God, but that he loved us, and sent
his Son to be the propitiation for our sins.
1 JOHN 4:9–10

Behold, what manner of love the Father hath bestowed upon us, that we should be called the sons of God.

1 JOHN 3:1

For I am persuaded, that neither death, nor life, nor angels, nor principalities, nor powers, nor things present, nor things to come, nor height, nor depth, nor any other creature, shall be able to separate us from the love of God, which is in Christ Jesus our Lord.

ROMANS 8:38–39

I am crucified with Christ: nevertheless I live; yet not I, but Christ liveth in me: and the life which I now live in the flesh I live by the faith of the Son of God, who loved me, and gave himself for me.

GALATIANS 2:20

Cause me to hear thy lovingkindness in the morning; for in thee do I trust: cause me to know the way wherein I should walk; for I lift up my soul unto thee.

PSALM 143:8

And walk in love, as Christ also hath loved us, and hath given himself for us an offering and a sacrifice to God for a sweetsmelling savour.

EPHESIANS 5:2

*For thou hast possessed my reins: thou hast covered me
in my mother's womb. I will praise thee; for I am fearfully
and wonderfully made: marvellous are thy works;
and that my soul knoweth right well. My substance was
not hid from thee, when I was made in secret, and curiously
wrought in the lowest parts of the earth. Thine eyes did
see my substance, yet being unperfect; and in thy book all
my members were written, which in continuance were
fashioned, when as yet there was none of them.*

PSALM 139:13–16

*That ye, being rooted and grounded in love, may be
able to comprehend with all saints what is the breadth,
and length, and depth, and height; and to know the
love of Christ, which passeth knowledge, that ye
might be filled with all the fulness of God.*

EPHESIANS 3:17–19

*Shew thy marvellous lovingkindness, O thou that
savest by thy right hand them which put their trust
in thee from those that rise up against them.*

PSALM 17:7

GOD'S PLAN FOR ME

When we're seeking healing, we're bombarded on all sides with "plans"—initial treatments, then backup strategies in case the previous ones fail. We may make our own private plans—"I want to be better by Christmas"—and then get discouraged if our recovery doesn't follow our hoped-for timetable. It can be so difficult to see what step to take next, let alone imagine the finish line. Thankfully, in uncertainty we still have hope in the Almighty. These Bible promises show that God has a redemptive plan for our lives—He will guide your steps as you trust in Him.

Trust in the LORD with all thine heart; and lean not unto thine own understanding. In all thy ways acknowledge him, and he shall direct thy paths.

PROVERBS 3:5–6

The steps of a good man are ordered by the LORD: and he delighteth in his way. Though he fall, he shall not be utterly cast down: for the LORD upholdeth him with his hand.

PSALM 37:23–24

*For I know the thoughts that I think toward you,
saith the LORD, thoughts of peace, and not of evil,
to give you an expected end. Then shall ye call upon
me, and ye shall go and pray unto me, and I will
hearken unto you. And ye shall seek me, and find me,
when ye shall search for me with all your heart.*

JEREMIAH 29:11–13

*For as the heavens are higher than the earth, so are my ways
higher than your ways, and my thoughts than your thoughts.*

ISAIAH 55:9

*For since the beginning of the world men have
not heard, nor perceived by the ear, neither hath
the eye seen, O God, beside thee, what he hath
prepared for him that waiteth for him.*

ISAIAH 64:4

*Many, O LORD my God, are thy wonderful works
which thou hast done, and thy thoughts which are to
us-ward: they cannot be reckoned up in order unto
thee: if I would declare and speak of them,
they are more than can be numbered.*

PSALM 40:5

And we know that all things work together for good to them that love God, to them who are the called according to his purpose. For whom he did foreknow, he also did predestinate to be conformed to the image of his Son, that he might be the firstborn among many brethren.

ROMANS 8:28–29

The LORD knoweth the days of the upright: and their inheritance shall be for ever.

PSALM 37:18

In whom also we have obtained an inheritance, being predestinated according to the purpose of him who worketh all things after the counsel of his own will: that we should be to the praise of his glory, who first trusted in Christ.

EPHESIANS 1:11–12

For we are his workmanship, created in Christ Jesus unto good works, which God hath before ordained that we should walk in them.

EPHESIANS 2:10

Know therefore that the LORD thy God, he is God,
the faithful God, which keepeth covenant and
mercy with them that love him and keep his
commandments to a thousand generations.

DEUTERONOMY 7:9

Remember the former things of old: for I am God, and there
is none else; I am God, and there is none like me, declaring
the end from the beginning, and from ancient times the
things that are not yet done, saying, My counsel shall
stand, and I will do all my pleasure.

ISAIAH 46:9–10

O house of Israel, cannot I do with you as this potter?
saith the LORD. Behold, as the clay is in the potter's
hand, so are ye in mine hand, O house of Israel.

JEREMIAH 18:6

For the LORD knoweth the way of the righteous:
but the way of the ungodly shall perish.

PSALM 1:6

Commit thy works unto the LORD, and thy thoughts
shall be established. The LORD hath made all things
for himself: yea, even the wicked for the day of evil.

PROVERBS 16:3–4

GOD'S POWER

The Creator that set the stars in place and filled the deepest oceans knows our names and our struggles. The same power that raised Jesus from the grave is working in the lives of all of us who believe in Him. He renews us daily, strengthening us to follow Christ faithfully in all circumstances. Nothing is impossible with God; He will bring restoration and beauty out of our pain, even if we don't receive complete healing in this life. If you feel powerless, reflect on these Bible promises about how you have access to God's infinite, loving power through Christ.

For the eyes of the LORD run to and fro throughout the whole earth, to shew himself strong in the behalf of them whose heart is perfect toward him.

2 CHRONICLES 16:9

The LORD reigneth, he is clothed with majesty; the LORD is clothed with strength, wherewith he hath girded himself: the world also is stablished, that it cannot be moved.

PSALM 93:1

For who is God save the LORD? or who is a rock save our God? It is God that girdeth me with strength, and maketh my way perfect. He maketh my feet like hinds' feet, and setteth me upon my high places.

PSALM 18:31–33

He hath made the earth by his power, he hath established the world by his wisdom, and hath stretched out the heavens by his discretion.

JEREMIAH 10:12

Lift up your eyes on high, and behold who hath created these things, that bringeth out their host by number: he calleth them all by names by the greatness of his might, for that he is strong in power; not one faileth.

ISAIAH 40:26

These things I have spoken unto you, that in me ye might have peace. In the world ye shall have tribulation: but be of good cheer; I have overcome the world.

JOHN 16:33

For though he was crucified through weakness, yet he liveth by the power of God. For we also are weak in him, but we shall live with him by the power of God toward you.

2 CORINTHIANS 13:4

*For by him were all things created, that are in heaven,
and that are in earth, visible and invisible, whether they
be thrones, or dominions, or principalities, or powers:
all things were created by him, and for him: and he is
before all things, and by him all things consist.*

COLOSSIANS 1:16–17

*And what is the exceeding greatness of his power to us-ward
who believe, according to the working of his mighty power,
which he wrought in Christ, when he raised him from the
dead, and set him at his own right hand in the heavenly
places, far above all principality, and power, and might,
and dominion, and every name that is named, not only in
this world, but also in that which is to come.*

EPHESIANS 1:19–21

*Now unto him that is able to do exceeding abundantly
above all that we ask or think, according to the power that
worketh in us, unto him be glory in the church by Christ
Jesus throughout all ages, world without end. Amen.*

EPHESIANS 3:20–21

*For I am not ashamed of the gospel of Christ: for it is
the power of God unto salvation to every one that
believeth; to the Jew first, and also to the Greek.*

ROMANS 1:16

*According as his divine power hath given unto us all things
that pertain unto life and godliness, through the knowledge
of him that hath called us to glory and virtue: whereby are
given unto us exceeding great and precious promises:
that by these ye might be partakers of the divine
nature, having escaped the corruption that
is in the world through lust.*

2 PETER 1:3–4

*Great is the LORD, and greatly to be praised;
and his greatness is unsearchable. One generation
shall praise thy works to another, and shall declare
thy mighty acts. I will speak of the glorious honour
of thy majesty, and of thy wondrous works.*

PSALM 145:3–5

*Behold, I am the LORD, the God of all flesh:
is there any thing too hard for me?*

JEREMIAH 32:27

GRATITUDE

Gratitude takes practice, especially during trials. But having a thankful attitude is more than just "the right thing to do"—it's a powerful agent for hope and healing too. Through gratitude, we choose to embrace God's blessings over focusing on the hard things, and our hearts remain soft toward Him. Practicing thankfulness can also help us be more confident in prayer; after naming God's faithful work we've seen in our lives, we're assured of His goodness and can bravely ask Him to show us more. These Bible promises show that God's people are blessed when their hearts overflow with thanksgiving.

Although the fig tree shall not blossom, neither shall fruit be in the vines; the labour of the olive shall fail, and the fields shall yield no meat; the flock shall be cut off from the fold, and there shall be no herd in the stalls: yet I will rejoice in the Lord, I will joy in the God of my salvation.
HABAKKUK 3:17–18

*Make a joyful noise unto the L*ORD*, all ye lands. Serve the* L*ORD with gladness: come before his presence with singing. Know ye that the* L*ORD he is God: it is he that hath made us, and not we ourselves; we are his people, and the sheep of his pasture. Enter into his gates with thanksgiving, and into his courts with praise: be thankful unto him, and bless his name. For the* L*ORD is good; his mercy is everlasting; and his truth endureth to all generations.*

PSALM 100:1–5

But be filled with the Spirit; speaking to yourselves in psalms and hymns and spiritual songs, singing and making melody in your heart to the Lord; giving thanks always for all things unto God and the Father in the name of our Lord Jesus Christ.

EPHESIANS 5:18–20

And whatsoever ye do in word or deed, do all in the name of the Lord Jesus, giving thanks to God and the Father by him.

COLOSSIANS 3:17

*And in that day shall ye say, Praise the L*ORD*, call upon his name, declare his doings among the people, make mention that his name is exalted. Sing unto the L*ORD*; for he hath done excellent things: this is known in all the earth.*

ISAIAH 12:4–5

*But I am poor and sorrowful: let thy salvation, O God,
set me up on high. I will praise the name of God with a
song, and will magnify him with thanksgiving.*

PSALM 69:29–30

*This is the day which the LORD hath made;
we will rejoice and be glad in it.*

PSALM 118:24

*Thou hast turned for me my mourning into dancing:
thou hast put off my sackcloth, and girded me with
gladness; to the end that my glory may sing praise
to thee, and not be silent. O LORD my God,
I will give thanks unto thee for ever.*

PSALM 30:11–12

*But thanks be to God, which giveth us the
victory through our Lord Jesus Christ.*

1 CORINTHIANS 15:57

*It is a good thing to give thanks unto the Lord, and to sing
praises unto thy name, O Most High: to shew forth thy
lovingkindness in the morning, and thy faithfulness every
night. For thou, Lord, hast made me glad through thy
work: I will triumph in the works of thy hands.*

PSALM 92:1–2, 4

Giving thanks unto the Father, which hath made us meet to
be partakers of the inheritance of the saints in light.
COLOSSIANS 1:12

By him therefore let us offer the sacrifice of
praise to God continually, that is, the fruit
of our lips giving thanks to his name.
HEBREWS 13:15

And let the peace of God rule in your hearts, to the which
also ye are called in one body; and be ye thankful.
COLOSSIANS 3:15

O give thanks unto the LORD, *for he is good: for his mercy*
endureth for ever. Let the redeemed of the LORD *say so,*
whom he hath redeemed from the hand of the enemy.
PSALM 107:1–2

GRIEF

Loss is one of the most painful experiences we can undergo in this life. We grieve for our loved ones who have died. We grieve for the abilities and activities that illness has taken from us. We weep for irreparable relationships. Loss hurts so much because creation wasn't meant to experience it—the Fall gave birth to death and sorrow. Jesus conquered death at the cross, but He too was touched by grief during His earthly life. These Bible promises remind us that Jesus understands our heart's deepest sorrow, and He will stay near us to give us comfort and hope.

Yea, though I walk through the valley of the shadow of death, I will fear no evil: for thou art with me; thy rod and thy staff they comfort me.

PSALM 23:4

Humble yourselves therefore under the mighty hand of God, that he may exalt you in due time: casting all your care upon him; for he careth for you.

1 PETER 5:6–7

*The LORD is nigh unto them that are of a broken
heart; and saveth such as be of a contrite spirit.
Many are the afflictions of the righteous:
but the LORD delivereth him out of them all.*

PSALM 34:18–19

*Blessed are they that mourn:
for they shall be comforted.*

MATTHEW 5:4

*Thou tellest my wanderings: put thou my tears into thy
bottle: are they not in thy book? In God will I praise his
word: in the LORD will I praise his word. In God have I put
my trust: I will not be afraid what man can do unto me.*

PSALM 56:8, 10–11

*Thy righteousness also, O God, is very high, who hast
done great things: O God, who is like unto thee!
Thou, which hast shewed me great and sore troubles,
shalt quicken me again, and shalt bring me up again
from the depths of the earth. Thou shalt increase
my greatness, and comfort me on every side.*

PSALM 71:19–21

My flesh and my heart faileth: but God is the
strength of my heart, and my portion for ever.
PSALM 73:26

Come unto me, all ye that labour and are
heavy laden, and I will give you rest.
MATTHEW 11:28

Blessed are ye that hunger now: for ye shall be filled.
Blessed are ye that weep now: for ye shall laugh.
LUKE 6:21

And God shall wipe away all tears from their eyes;
and there shall be no more death, neither sorrow,
nor crying, neither shall there be any more pain:
for the former things are passed away.
REVELATION 21:4

For the LORD shall comfort Zion: he will comfort all
her waste places; and he will make her wilderness
like Eden, and her desert like the garden of the
LORD; joy and gladness shall be found therein,
thanksgiving, and the voice of melody.
ISAIAH 51:3

Weeping may endure for a night,
but joy cometh in the morning.
PSALM 30:5

This is my comfort in my affliction:
for thy word hath quickened me.
PSALM 119:50

For this God is our God for ever and ever:
he will be our guide even unto death.
PSALM 48:14

So when this corruptible shall have put on incorruption,
and this mortal shall have put on immortality, then shall
be brought to pass the saying that is written, Death is
swallowed up in victory. O death, where is thy sting?
O grave, where is thy victory? The sting of death is sin;
and the strength of sin is the law. But thanks be to God,
which giveth us the victory through our Lord Jesus Christ.
1 CORINTHIANS 15:54–57

HEALING

We see miraculous healing in story after story in scripture. Jesus cast out demons, opened the eyes of the blind, cured leprosy, and raised the dead to life again. As we read, we're encouraged not just by Jesus' miraculous power but by what those healings signified—that He would heal us from our sins and restore our relationship with God. Just as we entrust our salvation to Him, we trust Him to heal our earthly bodies according to the Father's will. These Bible promises show that our compassionate Savior draws near to comfort, heal, and restore us.

Bless the LORD, O my soul, and forget not all his benefits: who forgiveth all thine iniquities; who healeth all thy diseases.

PSALM 103:2–3

In all their affliction he was afflicted, and the angel of his presence saved them: in his love and in his pity he redeemed them; and he bare them, and carried them all the days of old.

ISAIAH 63:9

When the even was come, they brought unto him many
that were possessed with devils: and he cast out the spirits
with his word, and healed all that were sick: that it might
be fulfilled which was spoken by Esaias the prophet, saying,
Himself took our infirmities, and bare our sicknesses.

MATTHEW 8:16–17

He healeth the broken in heart,
and bindeth up their wounds.

PSALM 147:3

The Spirit of the Lord GOD is upon me; because the
LORD hath anointed me to preach good tidings unto the
meek; he hath sent me to bind up the brokenhearted,
to proclaim liberty to the captives, and the opening of
the prison to them that are bound; to proclaim the
acceptable year of the LORD, and the day of vengeance
of our God; to comfort all that mourn.

ISAIAH 61:1–2

And Jesus went about all the cities and villages,
teaching in their synagogues, and preaching the
gospel of the kingdom, and healing every sickness
and every disease among the people.

MATTHEW 9:35

Surely he hath borne our griefs, and carried our sorrows:
yet we did esteem him stricken, smitten of God, and afflicted.
But he was wounded for our transgressions, he was bruised
for our iniquities: the chastisement of our peace was
upon him; and with his stripes we are healed.

ISAIAH 53:4–5

Then they cry unto the LORD in their trouble, and he saveth
them out of their distresses. He sent his word, and healed
them, and delivered them from their destructions.

PSALM 107:19–20

But unto you that fear my name shall the Sun of
righteousness arise with healing in his wings; and ye
shall go forth, and grow up as calves of the stall.

MALACHI 4:2

Then shall thy light break forth as the morning, and thine
health shall spring forth speedily: and thy righteousness shall
go before thee; the glory of the LORD shall be thy reward.

ISAIAH 58:8

For I will restore health unto thee, and I will heal thee of thy
wounds, saith the LORD; because they called thee an Outcast,
saying, This is Zion, whom no man seeketh after.

JEREMIAH 30:17

I have seen his ways, and will heal him: I will lead him also, and restore comforts unto him and to his mourners. I create the fruit of the lips; Peace, peace to him that is far off, and to him that is near, saith the Lord; and I will heal him.

ISAIAH 57:18–21

I will feed my flock, and I will cause them to lie down, saith the Lord GOD. I will seek that which was lost, and bring again that which was driven away, and will bind up that which was broken, and will strengthen that which was sick.

EZEKIEL 34:15–16

Is any among you afflicted? let him pray. Is any merry? let him sing psalms. Is any sick among you? let him call for the elders of the church; and let them pray over him, anointing him with oil in the name of the Lord: and the prayer of faith shall save the sick, and the Lord shall raise him up; and if he have committed sins, they shall be forgiven him.

JAMES 5:13–15

HOPE

Hope is more than a wish that things will turn out okay; it is living boldly with bravery and confidence. Hope stares down desperate situations and stands firm on God's promises— His faithfulness, His nearness, and His everlasting love and care for His children. On our healing journeys, it's essential for us to hold on to Christ and His promise that He will work all things out for our good. We don't have to wish that things are going to be okay; we *know* they will be. Reflect on these Bible promises that show how hope anchors us in tumultuous times.

For I know the thoughts that I think toward you,
saith the LORD, thoughts of peace, and not
of evil, to give you an expected end.
JEREMIAH 29:11

Now the God of hope fill you with all joy and
peace in believing, that ye may abound in hope,
through the power of the Holy Ghost.
ROMANS 15:13

Blessed be the God and Father of our Lord Jesus Christ,
which according to his abundant mercy hath begotten us
again unto a lively hope by the resurrection of Jesus Christ
from the dead, to an inheritance incorruptible, and undefiled,
and that fadeth not away, reserved in heaven for you.

1 PETER 1:3–4

For we know that the whole creation groaneth and
travaileth in pain together until now. And not only they,
but ourselves also, which have the firstfruits of the Spirit,
even we ourselves groan within ourselves, waiting for the
adoption, to wit, the redemption of our body. For we are
saved by hope: but hope that is seen is not hope: for what a
man seeth, why doth he yet hope for? But if we hope for
that we see not, then do we with patience wait for it.

ROMANS 8:22–25

The LORD is my portion, saith my soul;
therefore will I hope in him.

LAMENTATIONS 3:24

Hope deferred maketh the heart sick:
but when the desire cometh, it is a tree of life.

PROVERBS 13:12

For which cause we faint not; but though our outward man perish, yet the inward man is renewed day by day. For our light affliction, which is but for a moment, worketh for us a far more exceeding and eternal weight of glory; while we look not at the things which are seen, but at the things which are not seen: for the things which are seen are temporal; but the things which are not seen are eternal.

2 CORINTHIANS 4:16–18

Wherein God, willing more abundantly to shew unto the heirs of promise the immutability of his counsel, confirmed it by an oath: that by two immutable things, in which it was impossible for God to lie, we might have a strong consolation, who have fled for refuge to lay hold upon the hope set before us: which hope we have as an anchor of the soul, both sure and stedfast, and which entereth into that within the veil; whither the forerunner is for us entered, even Jesus, made an high priest for ever after the order of Melchisedec.

HEBREWS 6:17–20

He that goeth forth and weepeth, bearing precious seed, shall doubtless come again with rejoicing, bringing his sheaves with him.

PSALM 126:6

He will swallow up death in victory; and the Lord GOD will wipe away tears from off all faces; and the rebuke of his people shall he take away from off all the earth: for the LORD hath spoken it. And it shall be said in that day, Lo, this is our God; we have waited for him, and he will save us: this is the LORD; we have waited for him, we will be glad and rejoice in his salvation.

ISAIAH 25:8–9

Blessed is the man that trusteth in the LORD, and whose hope the LORD is. For he shall be as a tree planted by the waters, and that spreadeth out her roots by the river, and shall not see when heat cometh, but her leaf shall be green; and shall not be careful in the year of drought, neither shall cease from yielding fruit.

JEREMIAH 17:7–8

JOY

"Count it all joy," people say encouragingly, not knowing the true extent of what you're going through. Joy doesn't mean having a smile all the time—sometimes joy looks more like gritted teeth and silent, tearful prayer. Joy isn't happiness, but instead it's a deep confidence and an abiding sense of delight in our God. No matter our circumstances, joy bubbles to the surface when our hearts are centered in His beauty, strength, and love for us. These Bible promises are full of assurance that during the tough times, God gives us reason after reason to continue persevering in joy.

My brethren, count it all joy when ye fall into divers temptations; knowing this, that the trying of your faith worketh patience.
JAMES 1:2–3

Let all those that seek thee rejoice and be glad in thee: let such as love thy salvation say continually, The LORD be magnified.
PSALM 40:16

Although the fig tree shall not blossom, neither shall fruit be in the vines; the labour of the olive shall fail, and the fields shall yield no meat; the flock shall be cut off from the fold, and there shall be no herd in the stalls: Yet I will rejoice in the LORD, I will joy in the God of my salvation.

HABAKKUK 3:17–18

But let all those that put their trust in thee rejoice: let them ever shout for joy, because thou defendest them: let them also that love thy name be joyful in thee.

PSALM 5:11

Behold, God is my salvation; I will trust, and not be afraid: for the LORD JEHOVAH is my strength and my song; he also is become my salvation. Therefore with joy shall ye draw water out of the wells of salvation.

ISAIAH 12:2–3

Whom having not seen, ye love; in whom, though now ye see him not, yet believing, ye rejoice with joy unspeakable and full of glory: receiving the end of your faith, even the salvation of your souls.

1 PETER 1:8–9

A merry heart maketh a cheerful countenance:
but by sorrow of the heart the spirit is broken.
PROVERBS 15:13

I will sing unto the Lord as long as I live: I will sing
praise to my God while I have my being. My meditation
of him shall be sweet: I will be glad in the Lord.
PSALM 104:33–34

Delight thyself also in the LORD: and he
shall give thee the desires of thine heart.
PSALM 37:4

There be many that say, Who will shew us any good?
LORD, lift thou up the light of thy countenance upon us.
Thou hast put gladness in my heart, more than in the
time that their corn and their wine increased.
PSALM 4:6–7

All the days of the afflicted are evil: but he that
is of a merry heart hath a continual feast.
PROVERBS 15:15

I will bless the LORD at all times: his praise shall continually
be in my mouth. My soul shall make her boast in the
LORD: the humble shall hear thereof, and be glad.
PSALM 34:1–2

*Ye that love the L*ORD*, hate evil: he preserveth the
souls of his saints; he delivereth them out of the hand
of the wicked. Light is sown for the righteous,
and gladness for the upright in heart.*

PSALM 97:10–11

*Then shall the virgin rejoice in the dance,
both young men and old together: for I will turn
their mourning into joy, and will comfort them,
and make them rejoice from their sorrow.*

JEREMIAH 31:13

*How beautiful upon the mountains are the feet of
him that bringeth good tidings, that publisheth peace;
that bringeth good tidings of good, that publisheth
salvation; that saith unto Zion, Thy God reigneth!*

ISAIAH 52:7

*Blessed is the people that know the joyful sound:
they shall walk, O L*ORD*, in the light of thy countenance.
In thy name shall they rejoice all the day: and in
thy righteousness shall they be exalted.*

PSALM 89:15–16

LETTING GO OF THE PAST

It's hard to let go of shame and fear in our past, especially when we're haunted by terrible mistakes or have experienced horrible injustice. However long it takes, we need to let God's grace wash over these memories—there is nothing He cannot heal. If you struggle with regret, remember that Jesus has covered all your sins. For the deeply hurt, the Holy Spirit can move into the pained places of your heart and restore you by His comfort and grace. These Bible promises will encourage you to embrace the abundant life that Jesus gives when we trust in Him.

*Therefore if any man be in Christ, he is a
new creature: old things are passed away;
behold, all things are become new.*
2 Corinthians 5:17

*For as the heaven is high above the earth, so great is his
mercy toward them that fear him. As far as the east is from
the west, so far hath he removed our transgressions from us.*
Psalm 103:11–12

*Brethren, I count not myself to have apprehended:
but this one thing I do, forgetting those things which
are behind, and reaching forth unto those things
which are before, I press toward the mark for the
prize of the high calling of God in Christ Jesus.*
PHILIPPIANS 3:13–14

*I, even I, am he that blotteth out thy transgressions
for mine own sake, and will not remember thy sins.*
ISAIAH 43:25

*Therefore being justified by faith, we have peace
with God through our Lord Jesus Christ.*
ROMANS 5:1

*For godly sorrow worketh repentance to salvation not to be
repented of: but the sorrow of the world worketh death.*
2 CORINTHIANS 7:10

*I am crucified with Christ: nevertheless I live;
yet not I, but Christ liveth in me: and the life which
I now live in the flesh I live by the faith of the Son
of God, who loved me, and gave himself for me.*
GALATIANS 2:20

*Remember ye not the former things, neither consider the
things of old. Behold, I will do a new thing; now it shall
spring forth; shall ye not know it? I will even make a
way in the wilderness, and rivers in the desert.*

ISAIAH 43:18–19

*Fear not; for thou shalt not be ashamed: neither be thou
confounded; for thou shalt not be put to shame: for thou
shalt forget the shame of thy youth, and shalt not remember
the reproach of thy widowhood any more.*

ISAIAH 54:4

*For the LORD shall comfort Zion: he will comfort
all her waste places; and he will make her wilderness
like Eden, and her desert like the garden of the
LORD; joy and gladness shall be found therein,
thanksgiving, and the voice of melody.*

ISAIAH 51:3

*But now thus saith the Lord that created thee,
O Jacob, and he that formed thee, O Israel,
Fear not: for I have redeemed thee, I have
called thee by thy name; thou art mine.*

ISAIAH 43:1

*In the multitude of my thoughts within
me thy comforts delight my soul.*

PSALM 94:19

*To every thing there is a season, and a time to every
purpose under the heaven: a time to weep, and a time to
laugh; a time to mourn, and a time to dance; a time to get,
and a time to lose; a time to keep, and a time to cast away.*

ECCLESIASTES 3:1, 4, 6

*I sought the LORD, and he heard me, and delivered me
from all my fears. They looked unto him, and were
lightened: and their faces were not ashamed.*

PSALM 34:4–5

*Wherefore seeing we also are compassed about with so
great a cloud of witnesses, let us lay aside every weight,
and the sin which doth so easily beset us, and let us run with
patience the race that is set before us, looking unto Jesus the
author and finisher of our faith; who for the joy that was set
before him endured the cross, despising the shame, and is
set down at the right hand of the throne of God.*

HEBREWS 12:1–2

LONELINESS

On our healing journeys, we can feel extremely isolated, especially when people close to us don't know how to empathize with us. "How could they understand what I'm going through? They have such healthy, happy lives. I feel so alone in this." Jesus understands loneliness. He took on the ultimate isolation—separation from His beloved Father—to save us from our sins. Take courage from His name Emmanuel, which means "God with us." Ask Him for the comfort you need, whether it's understanding friends or a renewed sense of His presence. These Bible promises show that Emmanuel will never forsake you.

Whither shall I go from thy spirit? or whither shall I flee from thy presence? If I ascend up into heaven, thou art there: if I make my bed in hell, behold, thou art there. If I take the wings of the morning, and dwell in the uttermost parts of the sea; even there shall thy hand lead me, and thy right hand shall hold me.

Psalm 139:7–10

For what nation is there so great, who hath God
so nigh unto them, as the LORD our God is in
all things that we call upon him for?

DEUTERONOMY 4:7

Be strong and of a good courage, fear not, nor be afraid
of them: for the LORD thy God, he it is that doth go
with thee; he will not fail thee, nor forsake thee.

DEUTERONOMY 31:6

I have set the LORD always before me: because he is at my
right hand, I shall not be moved. Therefore my heart is glad,
and my glory rejoiceth: my flesh also shall rest in hope.

PSALM 16:8–9

They that trust in the Lord shall be as mount Zion, which
cannot be removed, but abideth for ever. As the mountains
are round about Jerusalem, so the Lord is round about
his people from henceforth even for ever.

PSALM 125:1–2

Whosoever shall confess that Jesus is the Son of God, God
dwelleth in him, and he in God. And we have known and
believed the love that God hath to us. God is love; and he
that dwelleth in love dwelleth in God, and God in him.

1 JOHN 4:15–16

For the LORD will not cast off his people,
neither will he forsake his inheritance.
PSALM 94:14

For I am persuaded, that neither death, nor life,
nor angels, nor principalities, nor powers, nor things
present, nor things to come, nor height, nor depth,
nor any other creature, shall be able to separate us from
the love of God, which is in Christ Jesus our Lord.
ROMANS 8:38–39

Lo, I am with you always,
even unto the end of the world.
MATTHEW 28:20

The LORD is nigh unto all them that call upon
him, to all that call upon him in truth. He will
fulfil the desire of them that fear him: he also
will hear their cry, and will save them.
PSALM 145:18–19

And the Word was made flesh, and dwelt among us,
(and we beheld his glory, the glory as of the only
begotten of the Father,) full of grace and truth.
JOHN 1:14

Am I a God at hand, saith the Lord, *and not a God afar off? Can any hide himself in secret places that I shall not see him? saith the* Lord. *Do not I fill heaven and earth? saith the* Lord.

Jeremiah 23:23–24

For thus saith the high and lofty One that inhabiteth eternity, whose name is Holy; I dwell in the high and holy place, with him also that is of a contrite and humble spirit, to revive the spirit of the humble, and to revive the heart of the contrite ones.

Isaiah 57:15

For the eyes of the Lord *run to and fro throughout the whole earth, to shew himself strong in the behalf of them whose heart is perfect toward him.*

2 Chronicles 16:9

For the eyes of the Lord are over the righteous, and his ears are open unto their prayers.

1 Peter 3:12

LOVING OTHERS

When we're in pain, it can be hard to continue showing love, whether it's to the people around us, to God, or even to ourselves. Our hearts can get so tangled up in our worries, emotions, and bodily pain that it's hard to believe our love is worth anything. Remember the Father's immeasurable love for you—He fills you with His abiding love when you feel you don't have any left. Dwell on these Bible promises, knowing that the love you give—even if it doesn't feel like much—pleases the Father and blesses those with whom you share it.

Charity suffereth long, and is kind; charity envieth not; charity vaunteth not itself, is not puffed up, doth not behave itself unseemly, seeketh not her own, is not easily provoked, thinketh no evil; rejoiceth not in iniquity, but rejoiceth in the truth; beareth all things, believeth all things, hopeth all things, endureth all things. Charity never faileth.

1 CORINTHIANS 13:4–8

Put on therefore, as the elect of God, holy and beloved,
bowels of mercies, kindness, humbleness of mind, meekness,
longsuffering; forbearing one another, and forgiving one
another, if any man have a quarrel against any: even as
Christ forgave you, so also do ye. And above all these things
put on charity, which is the bond of perfectness. And let
the peace of God rule in your hearts, to the which also
ye are called in one body; and be ye thankful.
COLOSSIANS 3:12–15

Jesus said unto him, Thou shalt love the Lord thy God
with all thy heart, and with all thy soul, and with all
thy mind. This is the first and great commandment.
And the second is like unto it, Thou shalt love thy
neighbour as thyself. On these two commandments
hang all the law and the prophets.
MATTHEW 22:37–40

Jesus answered and said unto him, If a man love me,
he will keep my words: and my Father will love him,
and we will come unto him, and make our abode with him.
JOHN 14:23

And the Lord direct your hearts into the love of God,
and into the patient waiting for Christ.
2 THESSALONIANS 3:5

Seeing ye have purified your souls in obeying the truth
through the Spirit unto unfeigned love of the brethren,
see that ye love one another with a pure heart fervently.
1 PETER 1:22

Finally, be ye all of one mind, having compassion one
of another, love as brethren, be pitiful, be courteous:
not rendering evil for evil, or railing for railing:
but contrariwise blessing; knowing that ye are
thereunto called, that ye should inherit a blessing.
1 PETER 3:8–9

This is my commandment, That ye love one another,
as I have loved you. Greater love hath no man than this,
that a man lay down his life for his friends.
JOHN 15:12–13

Be ye therefore followers of God, as dear children;
and walk in love, as Christ also hath loved us,
and hath given himself for us an offering and a
sacrifice to God for a sweetsmelling savour.
EPHESIANS 5:1–2

And above all things have fervent charity among
yourselves: for charity shall cover the multitude of sins.
1 PETER 4:8

Beloved, if God so loved us, we ought also to love one another. No man hath seen God at any time. If we love one another, God dwelleth in us, and his love is perfected in us.

1 John 4:11–12

And we have known and believed the love that God hath to us. God is love; and he that dwelleth in love dwelleth in God, and God in him. Herein is our love made perfect, that we may have boldness in the day of judgment: because as he is, so are we in this world.

1 John 4:16–17

There is no fear in love; but perfect love casteth out fear: because fear hath torment. He that feareth is not made perfect in love.

1 John 4:18

And the Lord make you to increase and abound in love one toward another, and toward all men, even as we do toward you.

1 Thessalonians 3:12

PEACE

The wind whips at our faces and the rain strikes us hard, yet during life's storms our hearts can be at peace if we've hidden them in Christ. We don't know what the next day or year will bring, or maybe we *do* know what hard things are coming, and we tremble at the thought. When we put our confidence in our trustworthy Savior, His peace fills and comforts us even as we see the dark clouds gathering. Read these Bible promises, and be encouraged that Jesus is the Source of abiding peace; He can calm us in any storm!

These things I have spoken unto you, that in me ye might have peace. In the world ye shall have tribulation: but be of good cheer; I have overcome the world.
JOHN 16:33

Peace I leave with you, my peace I give unto you: not as the world giveth, give I unto you. Let not your heart be troubled, neither let it be afraid.
JOHN 14:27

*God is our refuge and strength, a very present
help in trouble. Therefore will not we fear, though the
earth be removed, and though the mountains be carried
into the midst of the sea; though the waters thereof roar
and be troubled, though the mountains shake
with the swelling thereof. Selah.*

PSALM 46:1–3

*Thou wilt keep him in perfect peace, whose mind
is stayed on thee: because he trusteth in thee.*

ISAIAH 26:3

*For they that are after the flesh do mind the things of
the flesh; but they that are after the Spirit the things
of the Spirit. For to be carnally minded is death;
but to be spiritually minded is life and peace.*

ROMANS 8:5–6

*Be careful for nothing; but in every thing by prayer
and supplication with thanksgiving let your requests
be made known unto God. And the peace of God,
which passeth all understanding, shall keep your
hearts and minds through Christ Jesus.*

PHILIPPIANS 4:6–7

And let the peace of God rule in your hearts, to the which
also ye are called in one body; and be ye thankful.
Colossians 3:15

For ye shall go out with joy, and be led forth with peace:
the mountains and the hills shall break forth before you into
singing, and all the trees of the field shall clap their hands.
Isaiah 55:12

The Lord *bless thee, and keep thee: the* Lord *make his face*
shine upon thee, and be gracious unto thee: the Lord *lift*
up his countenance upon thee, and give thee peace.
Numbers 6:24–26

Now the Lord of peace himself give you peace
always by all means. The Lord be with you all.
2 Thessalonians 3:16

In the fear of the Lord *is strong confidence:*
and his children shall have a place of refuge.
Proverbs 14:26

I will both lay me down in peace, and sleep: for
thou, Lord, only makest me dwell in safety.
Psalm 4:8

Great peace have they which love thy law:
and nothing shall offend them.
PSALM 119:165

The LORD will give strength unto his people;
the LORD will bless his people with peace.
PSALM 29:11

But now in Christ Jesus ye who sometimes were far off
are made nigh by the blood of Christ. For he is our peace,
who hath made both one, and hath broken down the middle
wall of partition between us; having abolished in his flesh
the enmity, even the law of commandments contained in
ordinances; for to make in himself of twain one new man,
so making peace; and that he might reconcile both unto God
in one body by the cross, having slain the enmity thereby:
and came and preached peace to you which were afar off,
and to them that were nigh. For through him we
both have access by one Spirit unto the Father.
EPHESIANS 2:13–18

And the fruit of righteousness is sown
in peace of them that make peace.
JAMES 3:18

PERSEVERANCE

After so much work and time, we still might not see much progress in the mending of our bodies or the restoration of our broken relationships. It's so tempting to give up when it seems like nothing is improving. Don't give up—Jesus will help you continue on. Perseverance means choosing to trust Jesus and continue following Him even on the darkest, hardest days. These Bible promises will show you how God will provide what you need to persevere—His strength, and most importantly, His presence. No matter how long your journey is, remember that every step forward is a victory.

And not only so, but we glory in tribulations also: knowing that tribulation worketh patience; and patience, experience; and experience, hope: and hope maketh not ashamed; because the love of God is shed abroad in our hearts by the Holy Ghost which is given unto us.

ROMANS 5:3–5

Wherefore seeing we also are compassed about with so great a cloud of witnesses, let us lay aside every weight, and the sin which doth so easily beset us, and let us run with patience the race that is set before us, looking unto Jesus the author and finisher of our faith; who for the joy that was set before him endured the cross, despising the shame, and is set down at the right hand of the throne of God.

HEBREWS 12:1–2

Brethren, I count not myself to have apprehended: but this one thing I do, forgetting those things which are behind, and reaching forth unto those things which are before, I press toward the mark for the prize of the high calling of God in Christ Jesus.

PHILIPPIANS 3:13–14

Blessed is the man whose strength is in thee; in whose heart are the ways of them. Who passing through the valley of Baca make it a well; the rain also filleth the pools. They go from strength to strength, every one of them in Zion appeareth before God.

PSALM 84:5–7

And let us not be weary in well doing: for in due season we shall reap, if we faint not.

GALATIANS 6:9

And he said unto me, My grace is sufficient for thee:
for my strength is made perfect in weakness. Most gladly
therefore will I rather glory in my infirmities, that the
power of Christ may rest upon me.

2 Corinthians 12:9

Being confident of this very thing, that he which
hath begun a good work in you will perform
it until the day of Jesus Christ.

Philippians 1:6

Blessed is the man that endureth temptation: for when
he is tried, he shall receive the crown of life, which
the Lord hath promised to them that love him.

James 1:12

The Lord will perfect that which concerneth
me: thy mercy, O Lord, endureth for ever:
forsake not the works of thine own hands.

Psalm 138:8

Behold, we count them happy which endure. Ye have heard
of the patience of Job, and have seen the end of the Lord;
that the Lord is very pitiful, and of tender mercy.

James 5:11

*Therefore, brethren, stand fast, and hold the traditions
which ye have been taught, whether by word, or our epistle.
Now our Lord Jesus Christ himself, and God, even our
Father, which hath loved us, and hath given us everlasting
consolation and good hope through grace, comfort your
hearts, and stablish you in every good word and work.*

2 THESSALONIANS 2:15–17

*Him that overcometh will I make a pillar in the
temple of my God, and he shall go no more out: and I
will write upon him the name of my God, and the
name of the city of my God, which is new Jerusalem,
which cometh down out of heaven from my God:
and I will write upon him my new name.*

REVELATION 3:12

*Therefore, my beloved brethren, be ye stedfast, unmoveable,
always abounding in the work of the Lord, forasmuch as
ye know that your labour is not in vain in the Lord.*

1 CORINTHIANS 15:58

PRAYER

Prayer is one of the most precious gifts our heavenly Father has given us. Through Jesus, we are invited to come boldly into God's presence and tell Him everything that's going on in our lives. Prayer is a holy practice that is essential to our lives and our healing journey. Even if He doesn't change what's happening in our lives right away, through prayer and scripture God strengthens us to hold on to Him and His great love. Hold fast to these Bible promises as you come in humble faith to the Father and pour out all your needs before Him!

Because he hath inclined his ear unto me,
therefore will I call upon him as long as I live.
PSALM 116:2

I called upon thy name, O LORD, out of the low dungeon.
Thou hast heard my voice: hide not thine ear at my
breathing, at my cry. Thou drewest near in the day
that I called upon thee: thou saidst, Fear not.
LAMENTATIONS 3:55–57

*In my distress I called upon the L*ORD*, and cried unto*
my God: he heard my voice out of his temple, and
my cry came before him, even into his ears.
PSALM 18:6

And this is the confidence that we have in him, that,
if we ask any thing according to his will, he heareth us:
and if we know that he hear us, whatsoever we ask, we
know that we have the petitions that we desired of him.
1 JOHN 5:14–15

Let us therefore come boldly unto the throne of grace, that we
may obtain mercy, and find grace to help in time of need.
HEBREWS 4:16

And I say unto you, Ask, and it shall be given you; seek,
and ye shall find; knock, and it shall be opened unto you.
LUKE 11:9

Likewise the Spirit also helpeth our infirmities: for we
know not what we should pray for as we ought: but the
Spirit itself maketh intercession for us with groanings
which cannot be uttered. And he that searcheth the hearts
knoweth what is the mind of the Spirit, because he maketh
intercession for the saints according to the will of God.
ROMANS 8:26–27

Is any sick among you? let him call for the elders of the church; and let them pray over him, anointing him with oil in the name of the Lord: and the prayer of faith shall save the sick, and the Lord shall raise him up; and if he have committed sins, they shall be forgiven him.

JAMES 5:14–15

Call unto me, and I will answer thee, and show thee great and mighty things, which thou knowest not.

JEREMIAH 33:3

Rejoice evermore. Pray without ceasing. In every thing give thanks: for this is the will of God in Christ Jesus concerning you.

1 THESSALONIANS 5:16–18

For I know the thoughts that I think toward you, saith the Lord, thoughts of peace, and not of evil, to give you an expected end. Then shall ye call upon me, and ye shall go and pray unto me, and I will hearken unto you. And ye shall seek me, and find me, when ye shall search for me with all your heart.

JEREMIAH 29:11–13

The effectual fervent prayer of
a righteous man availeth much.
JAMES 5:16

And he spake a parable unto them to this end, that men
ought always to pray, and not to faint; saying, There was in
a city a judge, which feared not God, neither regarded man:
and there was a widow in that city; and she came unto him,
saying, Avenge me of mine adversary. And he would not for
a while: but afterward he said within himself, Though I fear
not God, nor regard man; yet because this widow troubleth
me, I will avenge her, lest by her continual coming she weary
me. And the Lord said, Hear what the unjust judge saith.
And shall not God avenge his own elect, which cry day and
night unto him, though he bear long with them? I tell you
that he will avenge them speedily. Nevertheless when the
Son of man cometh, shall he find faith on the earth?
LUKE 18:1–8

PROVISION

One of God's names is *Jehovah-jireh*, which means "The Lord Who Provides." Throughout scripture, we read about how God provided for the tangible and intangible needs of His people—He sent manna from heaven for the Israelites' hunger, and He sent Jesus to fill the spiritual hunger of our hearts. Through Christ, we can come before the Father boldly, carrying all our petitions for healing, for financial help, for strength to endure. He calls us to wait on Him in faith, but He doesn't leave His children desolate. These Bible promises show how God listens and answers His people's prayers for provision.

Therefore take no thought, saying, What shall we eat? or, What shall we drink? or, Wherewithal shall we be clothed? (For after all these things do the Gentiles seek:) for your heavenly Father knoweth that ye have need of all these things. But seek ye first the kingdom of God, and his righteousness; and all these things shall be added unto you.

MATTHEW 6:31–33

*The Lord is my shepherd; I shall not want. He maketh
me to lie down in green pastures: he leadeth me beside the
still waters. He restoreth my soul: he leadeth me in the
paths of righteousness for his name's sake.*

Psalm 23:1–3

*The eyes of all wait upon thee; and thou givest them
their meat in due season. Thou openest thine hand,
and satisfiest the desire of every living thing.*

Psalm 145:15–16

*But he answered and said, It is written, Man shall
not live by bread alone, but by every word that
proceedeth out of the mouth of God.*

Matthew 4:4

*I am the Lord thy God, which brought thee out of
the land of Egypt: open thy mouth wide, and I will fill it.
Oh that my people had hearkened unto me, and Israel
had walked in my ways! He should have fed them also
with the finest of the wheat: and with honey out
of the rock should I have satisfied thee.*

Psalm 81:10, 13, 16

But my God shall supply all your need according
to his riches in glory by Christ Jesus.
PHILIPPIANS 4:19

Ask ye of the Lord rain in the time of the latter rain;
so the Lord shall make bright clouds, and give them
showers of rain, to every one grass in the field.
ZECHARIAH 10:1

He causeth the grass to grow for the cattle, and herb
for the service of man: that he may bring forth food
out of the earth; and wine that maketh glad the heart
of man, and oil to make his face to shine,
and bread which strengtheneth man's heart.
PSALM 104:14–15

Behold, the Lord GOD will come with strong hand,
and his arm shall rule for him: behold, his reward is
with him, and his work before him. He shall feed
his flock like a shepherd: he shall gather the lambs
with his arm, and carry them in his bosom,
and shall gently lead those that are with young.
ISAIAH 40:10–11

But when ye pray, use not vain repetitions, as the heathen do: for they think that they shall be heard for their much speaking. Be not ye therefore like unto them: for your Father knoweth what things ye have need of, before ye ask him.

MATTHEW 6:7–8

And I say unto you, Ask, and it shall be given you; seek, and ye shall find; knock, and it shall be opened unto you. For every one that asketh receiveth; and he that seeketh findeth; and to him that knocketh it shall be opened. If a son shall ask bread of any of you that is a father, will he give him a stone? or if he ask a fish, will he for a fish give him a serpent? Or if he shall ask an egg, will he offer him a scorpion? If ye then, being evil, know how to give good gifts unto your children: how much more shall your heavenly Father give the Holy Spirit to them that ask him?

LUKE 11:9–13

Bless the LORD, O my soul, and forget not all his benefits: who satisfieth thy mouth with good things; so that thy youth is renewed like the eagle's.

PSALM 103:2, 5

QUESTIONING AND DOUBTS

When we are walking through pain, doubt and uncertainty can quietly creep in. "Why does God have me going through this? Right now I'm having a lot of trouble believing He's on my side." Thankfully, we can bring all of our questions, hurt, and doubts to Him. God can handle anything we ask Him, and He'll answer us wisely according to our need. Think of Gideon and his fleece (Judges 6), or Thomas declaring he needed to touch Jesus' wounds to believe (John 20). These Bible promises show that God will reach out to us in our doubt and give us hope.

Now the God of hope fill you with all joy and peace
in believing, that ye may abound in hope,
through the power of the Holy Ghost.
ROMANS 15:13

Humble yourselves therefore under the mighty hand
of God, that he may exalt you in due time: casting
all your care upon him; for he careth for you.
1 PETER 5:6–7

*Jesus said unto him, If thou canst believe, all things
are possible to him that believeth. And straightway
the father of the child cried out, and said with tears,
Lord, I believe; help thou mine unbelief.*

MARK 9:23–24

*Why sayest thou, O Jacob, and speakest, O Israel, My way
is hid from the LORD, and my judgment is passed over from
my God? Hast thou not known? hast thou not heard, that
the everlasting God, the LORD, the Creator of the ends of the
earth, fainteth not, neither is weary? there is no searching
of his understanding. He giveth power to the faint; and to
them that have no might he increaseth strength.*

ISAIAH 40:27–29

*I will say unto God my rock, Why hast thou forgotten me?
why go I mourning because of the oppression of the enemy?
As with a sword in my bones, mine enemies reproach me;
while they say daily unto me, Where is thy God? Why art
thou cast down, O my soul? and why art thou disquieted
within me? hope thou in God: for I shall yet praise him,
who is the health of my countenance, and my God.*

PSALM 42:9–11

And, behold, there arose a great tempest in the sea, insomuch that the ship was covered with the waves: but he was asleep. And his disciples came to him, and awoke him, saying, Lord, save us: we perish. And he saith unto them, Why are ye fearful, O ye of little faith? Then he arose, and rebuked the winds and the sea; and there was a great calm. But the men marvelled, saying, What manner of man is this, that even the winds and the sea obey him!

MATTHEW 8:24–27

But Thomas, one of the twelve, called Didymus, was not with them when Jesus came. The other disciples therefore said unto him, We have seen the Lord. But he said unto them, Except I shall see in his hands the print of the nails, and put my finger into the print of the nails, and thrust my hand into his side, I will not believe. And after eight days again his disciples were within, and Thomas with them: then came Jesus, the doors being shut, and stood in the midst, and said, Peace be unto you. Then saith he to Thomas, Reach hither thy finger, and behold my hands; and reach hither thy hand, and thrust it into my side: and be not faithless, but believing. And Thomas answered and said unto him, My Lord and my God. Jesus saith unto him, Thomas, because thou hast seen me, thou hast believed: blessed are they that have not seen, and yet have believed.

JOHN 20:24–29

*But Zion said, The L*ORD *hath forsaken me, and my Lord hath forgotten me. Can a woman forget her sucking child, that she should not have compassion on the son of her womb? yea, they may forget, yet will I not forget thee.*

ISAIAH 49:14–15

It is a faithful saying: for if we be dead with him, we shall also live with him: if we suffer, we shall also reign with him: if we deny him, he also will deny us: if we believe not, yet he abideth faithful: he cannot deny himself.

2 TIMOTHY 2:11–13

*I had fainted, unless I had believed to see the goodness of the L*ORD *in the land of the living. Wait on the L*ORD*: be of good courage, and he shall strengthen thine heart: wait, I say, on the L*ORD*.*

PSALM 27:13–14

QUESTIONING MY PURPOSE

Your whole world changes when you're going through extreme illness or trauma—old routines are traded in for doctor visits, treatments, and waiting for normalcy to return. If your condition persists, it's easy to question what your purpose is—"How can I do any good when I'm like this?" Though life has changed drastically, you are still an important part of God's family. These Bible promises show that God has planned out good work for you to do in His kingdom. Though you may feel limited, He'll give you wisdom to understand how to serve Him faithfully during this time.

For we are his workmanship, created in Christ Jesus unto good works, which God hath before ordained that we should walk in them.
EPHESIANS 2:10

And let us not be weary in well doing: for in due season we shall reap, if we faint not.
GALATIANS 6:9

Ye are the light of the world. A city that is set on an hill cannot be hid. Neither do men light a candle, and put it under a bushel, but on a candlestick; and it giveth light unto all that are in the house. Let your light so shine before men, that they may see your good works, and glorify your Father which is in heaven.

MATTHEW 5:14–16

Wherefore, my beloved, as ye have always obeyed, not as in my presence only, but now much more in my absence, work out your own salvation with fear and trembling. For it is God which worketh in you both to will and to do of his good pleasure.

PHILIPPIANS 2:12–13

For I know the thoughts that I think toward you, saith the LORD, thoughts of peace, and not of evil, to give you an expected end. Then shall ye call upon me, and ye shall go and pray unto me, and I will hearken unto you. And ye shall seek me, and find me, when ye shall search for me with all your heart.

JEREMIAH 29:11–13

*And God is able to make all grace abound toward
you; that ye, always having all sufficiency in all
things, may abound to every good work.*

2 Corinthians 9:8

*I am the vine, ye are the branches: He that abideth in
me, and I in him, the same bringeth forth much fruit: for
without me ye can do nothing. If ye abide in me, and my
words abide in you, ye shall ask what ye will, and it shall
be done unto you. Herein is my Father glorified, that ye
bear much fruit; so shall ye be my disciples.*

John 15:5, 7–8

*Blessed be God, even the Father of our Lord Jesus Christ,
the Father of mercies, and the God of all comfort; who
comforteth us in all our tribulation, that we may be able
to comfort them which are in any trouble, by the comfort
wherewith we ourselves are comforted of God.*

2 Corinthians 1:3–4

*Looking for that blessed hope, and the glorious
appearing of the great God and our Saviour Jesus
Christ; who gave himself for us, that he might
redeem us from all iniquity, and purify unto
himself a peculiar people, zealous of good works.*

Titus 2:13–14

*For God is not unrighteous to forget your work and labour
of love, which ye have shewed toward his name, in that
ye have ministered to the saints, and do minister.*

HEBREWS 6:10

*Trust in the LORD, and do good; so shalt thou dwell in the
land, and verily thou shalt be fed. Delight thyself also in
the LORD: and he shall give thee the desires of thine heart.*

PSALM 37:3–4

*And let the beauty of the LORD our God be upon us:
and establish thou the work of our hands upon us;
yea, the work of our hands establish thou it.*

PSALM 90:17

*I have planted, Apollos watered; but God gave the increase.
So then neither is he that planteth any thing, neither he
that watereth; but God that giveth the increase. Now he
that planteth and he that watereth are one: and every man
shall receive his own reward according to his own labour.
For we are labourers together with God: ye are God's
husbandry, ye are God's building.*

1 CORINTHIANS 3:6–9

RECONCILIATION

Reconciliation is seeking to restore a relationship that's been broken. Just as we follow Jesus' example for when we forgive others, we look to Him for reconciliation too—He brought us back to God through His sacrifice, and the Holy Spirit helps us to reconcile with one another. Sometimes it takes years for a relationship to heal. Sometimes reconciliation means that the relationship must end, but it ends in peace. Read these Bible promises, and be encouraged by your Savior's example, remembering that we depend on the power of the Spirit to heal relationships and change people's hearts.

And all things are of God, who hath reconciled us to himself by Jesus Christ, and hath given to us the ministry of reconciliation; to wit, that God was in Christ, reconciling the world unto himself, not imputing their trespasses unto them; and hath committed unto us the word of reconciliation.
2 Corinthians 5:18–19

And, having made peace through the blood of his cross,
by him to reconcile all things unto himself; by him, I say,
whether they be things in earth, or things in heaven.

COLOSSIANS 1:20

For if, when we were enemies, we were reconciled
to God by the death of his Son, much more,
being reconciled, we shall be saved by his life.

ROMANS 5:10

Follow peace with all men, and holiness, without which no
man shall see the Lord: looking diligently lest any man fail
of the grace of God; lest any root of bitterness springing
up trouble you, and thereby many be defiled.

HEBREWS 12:14–15

Therefore if thou bring thy gift to the altar, and there
rememberest that thy brother hath ought against thee;
leave there thy gift before the altar, and go thy way; first be
reconciled to thy brother, and then come and offer thy gift.

MATTHEW 5:23–24

Hatred stirreth up strifes: but love covereth all sins.

PROVERBS 10:12

If it be possible, as much as lieth in you,
live peaceably with all men.

ROMANS 12:18

Put on therefore, as the elect of God, holy and beloved,
bowels of mercies, kindness, humbleness of mind, meekness,
longsuffering; forbearing one another, and forgiving one
another, if any man have a quarrel against any: even as
Christ forgave you, so also do ye. And above all these things
put on charity, which is the bond of perfectness. And let the
peace of God rule in your hearts, to the which also ye
are called in one body; and be ye thankful.

COLOSSIANS 3:12–15

Moreover if thy brother shall trespass against thee, go and
tell him his fault between thee and him alone: if he shall
hear thee, thou hast gained thy brother. But if he will not
hear thee, then take with thee one or two more, that in
the mouth of two or three witnesses every word may be
established. And if he shall neglect to hear them, tell it unto
the church: but if he neglect to hear the church, let him
be unto thee as an heathen man and a publican.

MATTHEW 18:15–17

*Therefore judge nothing before the time, until the Lord
come, who both will bring to light the hidden things of
darkness, and will make manifest the counsels of the
hearts: and then shall every man have praise of God.*

1 CORINTHIANS 4:5

*Therefore all things whatsoever ye would that
men should do to you, do ye even so to them:
for this is the law and the prophets.*

MATTHEW 7:12

*Forbearing one another, and forgiving one
another, if any man have a quarrel against any:
even as Christ forgave you, so also do ye.*

COLOSSIANS 3:13

*Let no corrupt communication proceed out of your
mouth, but that which is good to the use of edifying,
that it may minister grace unto the hearers. And grieve
not the holy Spirit of God, whereby ye are sealed unto
the day of redemption. Let all bitterness, and wrath,
and anger, and clamour, and evil speaking, be put away
from you, with all malice: and be ye kind one to another,
tenderhearted, forgiving one another, even as
God for Christ's sake hath forgiven you.*

EPHESIANS 4:29–32

REPENTANCE

When we sin, repentance is necessary to heal the break in our relationship with God and those we've sinned against. When we repent, we choose to turn away from that sin, and our heart's desire is to never repeat it again, doing our best not to as we struggle with our sin nature on this side of heaven. As God's redeemed children, we please our holy Father when we repent and seek to follow His ways in our lives. In these Bible promises, you will see that when we repent, God is faithful and just to forgive us.

If we confess our sins, he is faithful and just to forgive us our sins, and to cleanse us from all unrighteousness.
1 JOHN 1:9

Have mercy upon me, O God, according to thy lovingkindness: according unto the multitude of thy tender mercies blot out my transgressions. Wash me throughly from mine iniquity, and cleanse me from my sin.
PSALM 51:1–2

Draw nigh to God, and he will draw nigh to you.
Cleanse your hands, ye sinners; and purify your hearts,
ye double minded. Be afflicted, and mourn, and weep:
let your laughter be turned to mourning, and your joy
to heaviness. Humble yourselves in the sight of
the Lord, and he shall lift you up.

JAMES 4:8–10

Withhold not thou thy tender mercies from me, O LORD:
let thy lovingkindness and thy truth continually preserve
me. For innumerable evils have compassed me about: mine
iniquities have taken hold upon me, so that I am not able
to look up; they are more than the hairs of mine head:
therefore my heart faileth me. Be pleased, O LORD,
to deliver me: O LORD, make haste to help me.

PSALM 40:11–13

For thou desirest not sacrifice; else would I give it:
thou delightest not in burnt offering. The sacrifices
of God are a broken spirit: a broken and a contrite
heart, O God, thou wilt not despise.

PSALM 51:16–17

He that covereth his sins shall not prosper: but whoso
confesseth and forsaketh them shall have mercy.

PROVERBS 28:13

And I will give them one heart, and I will put a new spirit within you; and I will take the stony heart out of their flesh, and will give them an heart of flesh: that they may walk in my statutes, and keep mine ordinances, and do them: and they shall be my people, and I will be their God.

EZEKIEL 11:19–20

The Lord is not slack concerning his promise, as some men count slackness; but is longsuffering to us-ward, not willing that any should perish, but that all should come to repentance.

2 PETER 3:9

Therefore also now, saith the LORD, turn ye even to me with all your heart, and with fasting, and with weeping, and with mourning: and rend your heart, and not your garments, and turn unto the LORD your God: for he is gracious and merciful, slow to anger, and of great kindness, and repenteth him of the evil.

JOEL 2:12–13

I say unto you, that likewise joy shall be in heaven over one sinner that repenteth, more than over ninety and nine just persons, which need no repentance.

LUKE 15:7

If my people, which are called by my name, shall humble themselves, and pray, and seek my face, and turn from their wicked ways; then will I hear from heaven, and will forgive their sin, and will heal their land.

2 CHRONICLES 7:14

Seek ye the LORD while he may be found, call ye upon him while he is near: let the wicked forsake his way, and the unrighteous man his thoughts: and let him return unto the LORD, and he will have mercy upon him; and to our God, for he will abundantly pardon.

ISAIAH 55:6–7

Sow to yourselves in righteousness, reap in mercy; break up your fallow ground: for it is time to seek the LORD, till he come and rain righteousness upon you.

HOSEA 10:12

REST

We crave physical and spiritual rest. It's such a comfort that we can rest in Jesus! To rest in Him means we set our worries aside to stand firm on His unchanging promises. Through His free gift of salvation, we have the unshakeable hope of eternity with Him. Here on earth, we know that He hears and answers us when we pray. When we surrender everything to Him—fears, dreams, and hopes—His rest permeates our hearts and gives solace to our bodies. Let these Bible promises fill you with confidence that Jesus provides heart-deep rest for His people.

Abide in me, and I in you. As the branch cannot bear fruit of itself, except it abide in the vine; no more can ye, except ye abide in me. I am the vine, ye are the branches: He that abideth in me, and I in him, the same bringeth forth much fruit: for without me ye can do nothing.

JOHN 15:4–5

*Come unto me, all ye that labour and are heavy laden,
and I will give you rest. Take my yoke upon you,
and learn of me; for I am meek and lowly in
heart: and ye shall find rest unto your souls.*

MATTHEW 11:28–29

*Hear my cry, O God; attend unto my prayer. From the
end of the earth will I cry unto thee, when my heart is
overwhelmed: lead me to the rock that is higher than I.
For thou hast been a shelter for me, and a strong tower
from the enemy. I will abide in thy tabernacle for ever:
I will trust in the covert of thy wings. Selah.*

PSALM 61:1–4

*My soul, wait thou only upon God; for my expectation
is from him. He only is my rock and my salvation:
he is my defence; I shall not be moved.*

PSALM 62:5–6

*Return unto thy rest, O my soul; for the LORD hath dealt
bountifully with thee. For thou hast delivered my soul from
death, mine eyes from tears, and my feet from falling.*

PSALM 116:7–8

The fear of the LORD tendeth to life: and he that hath it shall abide satisfied; he shall not be visited with evil.

PROVERBS 19:23

Rest in the Lord, and wait patiently for him: fret not thyself because of him who prospereth in his way, because of the man who bringeth wicked devices to pass.

PSALM 37:7

My little children, let us not love in word, neither in tongue; but in deed and in truth. And hereby we know that we are of the truth, and shall assure our hearts before him. For if our heart condemn us, God is greater than our heart, and knoweth all things.

1 JOHN 3:18–20

And he said, My presence shall go with thee, and I will give thee rest.

EXODUS 33:14

I have set the LORD always before me: because he is at my right hand, I shall not be moved. Therefore my heart is glad, and my glory rejoiceth: my flesh also shall rest in hope.

PSALM 16:8–9

There remaineth therefore a rest to the people of God.
For he that is entered into his rest, he also hath ceased
from his own works, as God did from his. Let us
labour therefore to enter into that rest, lest any
man fall after the same example of unbelief.
HEBREWS 4:9–11

The LORD is my shepherd; I shall not want. He maketh
me to lie down in green pastures: he leadeth me beside
the still waters. He restoreth my soul: he leadeth me
in the paths of righteousness for his name's sake.
PSALM 23:1–3

I will both lay me down in peace, and sleep:
for thou, LORD, only makest me dwell in safety.
PSALM 4:8

They that trust in the LORD shall be as mount Zion,
which cannot be removed, but abideth for ever. As the
mountains are round about Jerusalem, so the LORD is
round about his people from henceforth even for ever.
PSALM 125:1–2

REWRITING YOUR STORY

Our lives are intertwined in God's vast theme of redemption that we see woven in His Word. We can't simply brush our suffering aside, but we can search out His redemption in our healing journeys. We can choose to tell our stories through the vision of joy, with our eyes open to witness and retell God's mercy and goodness to us. We can reframe our painful tale in hope, trusting that God will show us the beauty He's bringing out of our circumstances. Meditate on these Bible promises about God's redemption, and take courage to begin rewriting your story.

Bless the LORD, O my soul: and all that is within me, bless his holy name. Bless the LORD, O my soul, and forget not all his benefits: who forgiveth all thine iniquities; who healeth all thy diseases; who redeemeth thy life from destruction; who crowneth thee with lovingkindness and tender mercies; who satisfieth thy mouth with good things; so that thy youth is renewed like the eagle's.

PSALM 103:1–5

And he that sat upon the throne said, Behold,
I make all things new. And he said unto me,
Write: for these words are true and faithful.
REVELATION 21:5

And I will give her her vineyards from thence, and the
valley of Achor for a door of hope: and she shall sing
there, as in the days of her youth, and as in the day
when she came up out of the land of Egypt.
HOSEA 2:15

Remember ye not the former things, neither consider the
things of old. Behold, I will do a new thing; now it shall
spring forth; shall ye not know it? I will even make a
way in the wilderness, and rivers in the desert.
ISAIAH 43:18–19

And I will restore to you the years that the locust hath
eaten, the cankerworm, and the caterpiller, and the
palmerworm, my great army which I sent among you.
And ye shall eat in plenty, and be satisfied, and praise the
name of the LORD your God, that hath dealt wondrously
with you: and my people shall never be ashamed.
JOEL 2:25–26

*They that sow in tears shall reap in joy. He that goeth forth
and weepeth, bearing precious seed, shall doubtless come
again with rejoicing, bringing his sheaves with him.*

PSALM 126:5–6

*And Joseph said unto them, Fear not: for am I in the
place of God? But as for you, ye thought evil against me;
but God meant it unto good, to bring to pass, as it is this
day, to save much people alive. Now therefore fear ye
not: I will nourish you, and your little ones. And he
comforted them, and spake kindly unto them.*

GENESIS 50:19–21

*Therefore we are buried with him by baptism into death:
that like as Christ was raised up from the dead by the glory
of the Father, even so we also should walk in newness of life.*

ROMANS 6:4

*As one whom his mother comforteth, so will I comfort you;
and ye shall be comforted in Jerusalem. And when ye see this,
your heart shall rejoice, and your bones shall flourish like an
herb: and the hand of the LORD shall be known toward his
servants, and his indignation toward his enemies.*

ISAIAH 66:13–14

And he hath put a new song in my mouth,
even praise unto our God: many shall see it,
and fear, and shall trust in the LORD.

PSALM 40:3

For the LORD thy God hath blessed thee in all the works
of thy hand: he knoweth thy walking through this great
wilderness: these forty years the LORD thy God hath
been with thee; thou hast lacked nothing.

DEUTERONOMY 2:7

To appoint unto them that mourn in Zion, to give
unto them beauty for ashes, the oil of joy for mourning,
the garment of praise for the spirit of heaviness; that they
might be called trees of righteousness, the planting
of the LORD, that he might be glorified.

ISAIAH 61:3

SALVATION

Our salvation through Christ is the bedrock of our lives and our hope for the future. He conquered sin and death by the power of His resurrection, and that same life-giving power moves in our lives. We don't have to fear what may happen in life, because He's promised to walk it with us. We don't have to fear death because our salvation is secure, and Jesus will help us make that crossing when it's time. When you need assurance, remember these Bible promises—no matter what happens, nothing can snatch you out of the Father's hand.

Blessed be the God and Father of our Lord Jesus Christ, which according to his abundant mercy hath begotten us again unto a lively hope by the resurrection of Jesus Christ from the dead, to an inheritance incorruptible, and undefiled, and that fadeth not away, reserved in heaven for you, who are kept by the power of God through faith unto salvation ready to be revealed in the last time.

1 PETER 1:3–5

For God so loved the world, that he gave his only begotten
Son, that whosoever believeth in him should not perish,
but have everlasting life. For God sent not his Son into
the world to condemn the world; but that the
world through him might be saved.

JOHN 3:16–17

Verily, verily, I say unto you, He that heareth
my word, and believeth on him that sent me,
hath everlasting life, and shall not come into
condemnation; but is passed from death unto life.

JOHN 5:24

My sheep hear my voice, and I know them, and they follow
me: and I give unto them eternal life; and they shall never
perish, neither shall any man pluck them out of my hand.
My Father, which gave them me, is greater than all;
and no man is able to pluck them out of my Father's hand.

JOHN 10:27–29

That if thou shalt confess with thy mouth the Lord Jesus,
and shalt believe in thine heart that God hath raised
him from the dead, thou shalt be saved. For with the
heart man believeth unto righteousness; and with
the mouth confession is made unto salvation.

ROMANS 10:9–10

Jesus answered and said unto her, Whosoever drinketh of
this water shall thirst again: but whosoever drinketh of
the water that I shall give him shall never thirst; but the
water that I shall give him shall be in him a well
of water springing up into everlasting life.
John 4:13–14

But ye are a chosen generation, a royal priesthood,
an holy nation, a peculiar people; that ye should shew forth
the praises of him who hath called you out of darkness into
his marvellous light; which in time past were not a people,
but are now the people of God: which had not obtained
mercy, but now have obtained mercy.
1 Peter 2:9–10

Behold, God is my salvation; I will trust, and not be
afraid: for the Lord Jehovah is my strength and
my song; he also is become my salvation.
Isaiah 12:2

There is therefore now no condemnation to them which are
in Christ Jesus, who walk not after the flesh, but after the
Spirit. For the law of the Spirit of life in Christ Jesus
hath made me free from the law of sin and death.
Romans 8:1–2

*Jesus said unto her, I am the resurrection, and the
life: he that believeth in me, though he were dead,
yet shall he live: and whosoever liveth and believeth
in me shall never die. Believest thou this?*

JOHN 11:25–26

*For by grace are ye saved through faith; and that
not of yourselves: it is the gift of God: not of
works, lest any man should boast.*

EPHESIANS 2:8–9

*So when this corruptible shall have put on incorruption,
and this mortal shall have put on immortality, then shall
be brought to pass the saying that is written, Death is
swallowed up in victory. O death, where is thy sting?
O grave, where is thy victory? The sting of death is sin;
and the strength of sin is the law. But thanks be
to God, which giveth us the victory
through our Lord Jesus Christ.*

1 CORINTHIANS 15:54–57

SHAME

Shame is that small, sinister voice in your heart that whispers to you that you're deeply flawed and undeserving of love. "If they knew what you're *really* like. . .if they knew what you've done. . ." Shame makes you want to hide, but you don't have to. When Jesus saved you, He took on your shame as well as your sin. Neither your past nor present failings can undo the fact that Jesus has made you a new creation! Absorb these Bible promises so when you hear shame's whispering voice you can answer with the truth: "In Christ, I am loved and redeemed."

Bless the LORD, O my soul: and all that is within me, bless his holy name. Bless the LORD, O my soul, and forget not all his benefits: who forgiveth all thine iniquities; who healeth all thy diseases; who redeemeth thy life from destruction; who crowneth thee with lovingkindness and tender mercies; who satisfieth thy mouth with good things; so that thy youth is renewed like the eagle's.

PSALM 103:1–5

There is therefore now no condemnation to them which are in Christ Jesus, who walk not after the flesh, but after the Spirit. For the law of the Spirit of life in Christ Jesus hath made me free from the law of sin and death.

ROMANS 8:1–2

I will greatly rejoice in the LORD, my soul shall be joyful in my God; for he hath clothed me with the garments of salvation, he hath covered me with the robe of righteousness, as a bridegroom decketh himself with ornaments, and as a bride adorneth herself with her jewels.

ISAIAH 61:10

Now the Lord is that Spirit: and where the Spirit of the Lord is, there is liberty. But we all, with open face beholding as in a glass the glory of the Lord, are changed into the same image from glory to glory, even as by the Spirit of the Lord.

2 CORINTHIANS 3:17–18

Come now, and let us reason together, saith the LORD: though your sins be as scarlet, they shall be as white as snow; though they be red like crimson, they shall be as wool.

ISAIAH 1:18

I will praise thee; for I am fearfully and
wonderfully made: marvellous are thy works;
and that my soul knoweth right well.

PSALM 139:14

(For the weapons of our warfare are not carnal, but mighty
through God to the pulling down of strong holds;) casting
down imaginations, and every high thing that exalteth
itself against the knowledge of God, and bringing into
captivity every thought to the obedience of Christ.

2 CORINTHIANS 10:4–5

Finally, brethren, whatsoever things are true,
whatsoever things are honest, whatsoever things are just,
whatsoever things are pure, whatsoever things are lovely,
whatsoever things are of good report; if there be any virtue,
and if there be any praise, think on these things.

PHILIPPIANS 4:8

As ye have therefore received Christ Jesus the Lord,
so walk ye in him: rooted and built up in him,
and stablished in the faith, as ye have been taught,
abounding therein with thanksgiving.

COLOSSIANS 2:6–7

Even as Christ also loved the church, and gave himself for it; that he might sanctify and cleanse it with the washing of water by the word, that he might present it to himself a glorious church, not having spot, or wrinkle, or any such thing; but that it should be holy and without blemish.

EPHESIANS 5:25–27

Fear not; for thou shalt not be ashamed: neither be thou confounded; for thou shalt not be put to shame: for thou shalt forget the shame of thy youth, and shalt not remember the reproach of thy widowhood any more. For thy Maker is thine husband; the LORD of hosts is his name; and thy Redeemer the Holy One of Israel; the God of the whole earth shall he be called.

ISAIAH 54:4–5

My little children, let us not love in word, neither in tongue; but in deed and in truth. And hereby we know that we are of the truth, and shall assure our hearts before him. For if our heart condemn us, God is greater than our heart, and knoweth all things. Beloved, if our heart condemn us not, then have we confidence toward God.

1 JOHN 3:18–21

STRENGTH

Stress saps our strength when we face a multitude of troubles—medical bills, heavy family obligations, persistent pain, sleepless nights. God doesn't expect us to accomplish everything on our own. He also doesn't ask us to "do the best we can" and only after we're exhausted will He step in to assist. God promises His nearness in every moment of our lives and gives us grace to trust that He will generously provide strength to us in our time of need. In these Bible promises, we see how God continually strengthens those who have put their confidence in Him.

Be strong and of a good courage; be not afraid,
neither be thou dismayed: for the LORD thy God
is with thee whithersoever thou goest.
JOSHUA 1:9

The LORD God is my strength, and he will make
my feet like hinds' feet, and he will make
me to walk upon mine high places.
HABAKKUK 3:19

Hast thou not known? hast thou not heard,
that the everlasting God, the LORD, *the Creator of*
the ends of the earth, fainteth not, neither is weary?
there is no searching of his understanding. He giveth
power to the faint; and to them that have no might he
increaseth strength. Even the youths shall faint and be
weary, and the young men shall utterly fall: but they that
wait upon the LORD *shall renew their strength; they shall*
mount up with wings as eagles; they shall run, and not
be weary; and they shall walk, and not faint.

ISAIAH 40:28–31

I will love thee, O LORD, *my strength. The* LORD *is*
my rock, and my fortress, and my deliverer; my God,
my strength, in whom I will trust; my buckler, and
the horn of my salvation, and my high tower.

PSALM 18:1–2

Fear thou not; for I am with thee: be not dismayed; for I am
thy God: I will strengthen thee; yea, I will help thee; yea,
I will uphold thee with the right hand of my righteousness.

ISAIAH 41:10

Seek the LORD *and his strength, seek his face continually.*

1 CHRONICLES 16:11

The righteous cry, and the LORD heareth,
and delivereth them out of all their troubles.
PSALM 34:17

But the God of all grace, who hath called us unto his eternal
glory by Christ Jesus, after that ye have suffered a while,
make you perfect, stablish, strengthen, settle you.
1 PETER 5:10

O love the LORD, all ye his saints: for the LORD preserveth
the faithful, and plentifully rewardeth the proud doer.
Be of good courage, and he shall strengthen your
heart, all ye that hope in the LORD.
PSALM 31:23–24

Some trust in chariots, and some in horses: but we
will remember the name of the LORD our God.
PSALM 20:7

I can do all things through Christ which strengtheneth me.
PHILIPPIANS 4:13

The LORD is my light and my salvation;
whom shall I fear? the LORD is the strength
of my life; of whom shall I be afraid?
PSALM 27:1

For who is God save the LORD? or who is a
rock save our God? It is God that girdeth me
with strength, and maketh my way perfect.
PSALM 18:31–32

Finally, my brethren, be strong in the Lord, and in the
power of his might. Put on the whole armour of God,
that ye may be able to stand against the wiles of the devil.
For we wrestle not against flesh and blood, but against
principalities, against powers, against the rulers of the
darkness of this world, against spiritual wickedness in
high places. Wherefore take unto you the whole armour
of God, that ye may be able to withstand in the evil day,
and having done all, to stand. Stand therefore, having your
loins girt about with truth, and having on the breastplate
of righteousness; and your feet shod with the preparation
of the gospel of peace; above all, taking the shield
of faith, wherewith ye shall be able to quench
all the fiery darts of the wicked.
EPHESIANS 6:10–16

SUFFERING

How do we cope with suffering? The Bible is filled with promises for those who suffer—our suffering is not meaningless, and we can learn to follow Christ better through our painful experiences. Jesus endured physical pain, emotional distress, and spiritual devastation when He was separated from His Father on the cross, yet He remained obedient. Our Savior understands what we feel and will comfort us, giving us the strength to persevere. May these Bible promises fill you with hope—for consolation through the Spirit and strength to endure until God's glorious purpose for us is revealed.

And we know that all things work together for good to them that love God, to them who are the called according to his purpose. For whom he did foreknow, he also did predestinate to be conformed to the image of his Son, that he might be the firstborn among many brethren.
ROMANS 8:28–29

For which cause we faint not; but though our outward man perish, yet the inward man is renewed day by day. For our light affliction, which is but for a moment, worketh for us a far more exceeding and eternal weight of glory; while we look not at the things which are seen, but at the things which are not seen: for the things which are seen are temporal; but the things which are not seen are eternal.

2 CORINTHIANS 4:16–18

Take, my brethren, the prophets, who have spoken in the name of the Lord, for an example of suffering affliction, and of patience. Behold, we count them happy which endure. Ye have heard of the patience of Job, and have seen the end of the Lord; that the Lord is very pitiful, and of tender mercy.

JAMES 5:10–11

And not only so, but we glory in tribulations also: knowing that tribulation worketh patience; and patience, experience; and experience, hope: and hope maketh not ashamed; because the love of God is shed abroad in our hearts by the Holy Ghost which is given unto us.

ROMANS 5:3–5

*Wherefore let them that suffer according to the will
of God commit the keeping of their souls to him
in well doing, as unto a faithful Creator.*
1 PETER 4:19

*And lest I should be exalted above measure through the
abundance of the revelations, there was given to me a thorn
in the flesh, the messenger of Satan to buffet me, lest I should
be exalted above measure. For this thing I besought the
Lord thrice, that it might depart from me. And he said unto
me, My grace is sufficient for thee: for my strength is made
perfect in weakness. Most gladly therefore will I rather glory
in my infirmities, that the power of Christ may rest upon
me. Therefore I take pleasure in infirmities, in reproaches,
in necessities, in persecutions, in distresses for Christ's
sake: for when I am weak, then am I strong.*
2 CORINTHIANS 12:7–10

*For I reckon that the sufferings of this present
time are not worthy to be compared with
the glory which shall be revealed in us.*
ROMANS 8:18

But if, when ye do well, and suffer for it, ye take it patiently,
this is acceptable with God. For even hereunto were ye
called: because Christ also suffered for us, leaving us an
example, that ye should follow his steps: who did
no sin, neither was guile found in his mouth.

1 PETER 2:20–22

For I know that my redeemer liveth, and that he shall stand
at the latter day upon the earth: and though after my skin
worms destroy this body, yet in my flesh shall I see God:
whom I shall see for myself, and mine eyes shall behold,
and not another; though my reins be consumed within me.

JOB 19:25–27

The sorrows of death compassed me, and the pains of hell
gat hold upon me: I found trouble and sorrow. Then called
I upon the name of the LORD; O LORD, I beseech thee,
deliver my soul. Gracious is the LORD, and righteous;
yea, our God is merciful. The LORD preserveth the
simple: I was brought low, and he helped me.

PSALM 116:3–6

TEMPTATION

In the moment we are tempted, we must choose—will we decide to obey God or to turn away from what pleases Him? On our healing journeys, temptation can come from all sides—we might be tempted to be angry with God or to despair, or to react to our pain by hurting those around us. Just as God is gracious to forgive us, He also gives us grace for our times of temptation. Read these Bible promises that show how God provided a way to combat temptation and Satan's lies by giving us His true Word to guide us.

Blessed is the man that endureth temptation:
for when he is tried, he shall receive the crown of life,
which the Lord hath promised to them that love him.

JAMES 1:12

There hath no temptation taken you but such as is common
to man: but God is faithful, who will not suffer you to be
tempted above that ye are able; but will with the temptation
also make a way to escape, that ye may be able to bear it.

1 CORINTHIANS 10:13

Let no man say when he is tempted, I am tempted of
God: for God cannot be tempted with evil, neither
tempteth he any man: but every man is tempted,
when he is drawn away of his own lust, and enticed.
Then when lust hath conceived, it bringeth forth sin:
and sin, when it is finished, bringeth forth death.
JAMES 1:13–15

Submit yourselves therefore to God.
Resist the devil, and he will flee from you.
JAMES 4:7

The Lord knoweth how to deliver the godly out of
temptations, and to reserve the unjust unto
the day of judgment to be punished.
2 PETER 2:9

Seeing then that we have a great high priest, that is passed
into the heavens, Jesus the Son of God, let us hold fast our
profession. For we have not an high priest which cannot
be touched with the feeling of our infirmities; but was in
all points tempted like as we are, yet without sin. Let us
therefore come boldly unto the throne of grace, that we may
obtain mercy, and find grace to help in time of need.
HEBREWS 4:14–16

When wisdom entereth into thine heart, and knowledge
is pleasant unto thy soul; discretion shall preserve thee,
understanding shall keep thee: to deliver thee from the way
of the evil man, from the man that speaketh froward things.

PROVERBS 2:10–12

For in that he [Christ] himself hath suffered being tempted,
he is able to succour them that are tempted.

HEBREWS 2:18

He that walketh righteously, and speaketh uprightly; he
that despiseth the gain of oppressions, that shaketh his hands
from holding of bribes, that stoppeth his ears from hearing of
blood, and shutteth his eyes from seeing evil; he shall dwell
on high: his place of defence shall be the munitions of rocks:
bread shall be given him; his waters shall be sure.

ISAIAH 33:15–16

Let not sin therefore reign in your mortal body, that ye
should obey it in the lusts thereof. Neither yield ye your
members as instruments of unrighteousness unto sin: but
yield yourselves unto God, as those that are alive from the
dead, and your members as instruments of righteousness
unto God. For sin shall not have dominion over you:
for ye are not under the law, but under grace.

ROMANS 6:12–14

But as for me, my feet were almost gone; my steps had well nigh slipped. For I was envious at the foolish, when I saw the prosperity of the wicked. Until I went into the sanctuary of God; then understood I their end. Surely thou didst set them in slippery places: thou castedst them down into destruction. How are they brought into desolation, as in a moment! They are utterly consumed with terrors. Thus my heart was grieved, and I was pricked in my reins. So foolish was I, and ignorant: I was as a beast before thee. Nevertheless I am continually with thee: thou hast holden me by my right hand. Thou shalt guide me with thy counsel, and afterward receive me to glory.

PSALM 73:2–3, 17–19, 21–24

TRIALS

The Bible warns us not to be surprised when trials come, but that doesn't make them any less difficult to bear. Some trials are the result of persecution; others are evidence of the broken world we live in—natural disasters, a sudden loss, chronic illnesses. As you look at these promises from God's Word, remember that He assures us that our trials have a purpose—when we walk with Him, troubled times transform us more and more into the image of Christ. In the midst of hardship, our Savior will provide us the strength and courage to endure with joy.

My brethren, count it all joy when ye fall into divers temptations; knowing this, that the trying of your faith worketh patience.
JAMES 1:2–3

These things I have spoken unto you, that in me ye might have peace. In the world ye shall have tribulation: but be of good cheer; I have overcome the world.
JOHN 16:33

Beloved, think it not strange concerning the fiery trial which is to try you, as though some strange thing happened unto you: but rejoice, inasmuch as ye are partakers of Christ's sufferings; that, when his glory shall be revealed, ye may be glad also with exceeding joy.

1 PETER 4:12–13

Blessed is the man that endureth temptation: for when he is tried, he shall receive the crown of life, which the Lord hath promised to them that love him.

JAMES 1:12

Wherein ye greatly rejoice, though now for a season, if need be, ye are in heaviness through manifold temptations: that the trial of your faith, being much more precious than of gold that perisheth, though it be tried with fire, might be found unto praise and honour and glory at the appearing of Jesus Christ.

1 PETER 1:6–7

For whatsoever is born of God overcometh the world: and this is the victory that overcometh the world, even our faith. Who is he that overcometh the world, but he that believeth that Jesus is the Son of God?

1 JOHN 5:4–5

And not only so, but we glory in tribulations also: knowing
that tribulation worketh patience; and patience, experience;
and experience, hope: and hope maketh not ashamed;
because the love of God is shed abroad in our hearts
by the Holy Ghost which is given unto us.
ROMANS 5:3–5

But now thus saith the LORD that created thee, O Jacob,
and he that formed thee, O Israel, Fear not: for I have
redeemed thee, I have called thee by thy name; thou art
mine. When thou passest through the waters, I will be
with thee; and through the rivers, they shall not overflow
thee: when thou walkest through the fire, thou shalt not
be burned; neither shall the flame kindle upon thee.
ISAIAH 43:1–2

Therefore whosoever heareth these sayings of mine, and
doeth them, I will liken him unto a wise man, which built
his house upon a rock: and the rain descended, and the floods
came, and the winds blew, and beat upon that house;
and it fell not: for it was founded upon a rock.
MATTHEW 7:24–25

*Blessed be God, even the Father of our Lord Jesus
Christ, the Father of mercies, and the God of all comfort;
who comforteth us in all our tribulation, that we may
be able to comfort them which are in any trouble, by the
comfort wherewith we ourselves are comforted of God.
For as the sufferings of Christ abound in us, so our
consolation also aboundeth by Christ.*

2 CORINTHIANS 1:3–5

*And I will bring the third part through the fire,
and will refine them as silver is refined, and will try
them as gold is tried: they shall call on my name,
and I will hear them: I will say, It is my people:
and they shall say, The LORD is my God.*

ZECHARIAH 13:9

*We are troubled on every side, yet not distressed; we are
perplexed, but not in despair; persecuted, but not forsaken;
cast down, but not destroyed; always bearing about in the
body the dying of the Lord Jesus, that the life also of Jesus
might be made manifest in our body. For we which live are
always delivered unto death for Jesus' sake, that the life also
of Jesus might be made manifest in our mortal flesh.*

2 CORINTHIANS 4:8–11

UNWORTHINESS

When we don't function the way we want to—whether we are newly hurt or recovering—it's easy to look at the healthy "norm" and feel unworthy. "I'm so hard to be around. I'm such a burden." We might feel like we don't deserve others' love and attention. But Christ doesn't measure us by what we can accomplish physically or handle emotionally. He looks at us with the same love that moved Him to come to earth to save us. These Bible promises show that you are complete, worthy, and accepted in Jesus—embrace His profound love when you feel unlovable.

The LORD hath appeared of old unto me, saying,
Yea, I have loved thee with an everlasting love:
therefore with lovingkindness have I drawn thee.
JEREMIAH 31:3

Know ye that the LORD he is God: it is he that
hath made us, and not we ourselves; we are
his people, and the sheep of his pasture.
PSALM 100:3

For by grace are ye saved through faith;
and that not of yourselves: it is the gift of God:
not of works, lest any man should boast.

EPHESIANS 2:8–9

Blessed be the God and Father of our Lord Jesus Christ, who
hath blessed us with all spiritual blessings in heavenly places
in Christ: according as he hath chosen us in him before the
foundation of the world, that we should be holy and without
blame before him in love: having predestinated us unto the
adoption of children by Jesus Christ to himself, according
to the good pleasure of his will, to the praise of the glory
of his grace, wherein he hath made us accepted in the
beloved. In whom we have redemption through his blood,
the forgiveness of sins, according to the riches of his grace.

EPHESIANS 1:3–7

The Lord thy God in the midst of thee is mighty;
he will save, he will rejoice over thee with joy; he will
rest in his love, he will joy over thee with singing.

ZEPHANIAH 3:17

Behold, what manner of love the Father hath bestowed
upon us, that we should be called the sons of God.

1 JOHN 3:1

For ye have not received the spirit of bondage again to fear;
but ye have received the Spirit of adoption, whereby we cry,
Abba, Father. The Spirit itself beareth witness with our
spirit, that we are the children of God: and if children, then
heirs; heirs of God, and joint-heirs with Christ; if so be that
we suffer with him, that we may be also glorified together.
ROMANS 8:15–17

I will say to the north, Give up; and to the south,
Keep not back: bring my sons from far, and my daughters
from the ends of the earth; even every one that is called
by my name: for I have created him for my glory,
I have formed him; yea, I have made him.
ISAIAH 43:6–7

Now therefore ye are no more strangers and foreigners,
but fellowcitizens with the saints, and of the household of
God; and are built upon the foundation of the apostles and
prophets, Jesus Christ himself being the chief corner stone;
in whom all the building fitly framed together groweth unto
an holy temple in the Lord: in whom ye also are builded
together for an habitation of God through the Spirit.
EPHESIANS 2:19–22

Blessed are the poor in spirit:
for theirs is the kingdom of heaven.
MATTHEW 5:3

And they shall call them, The holy people,
The redeemed of the LORD: and thou shalt
be called, Sought out, A city not forsaken.
ISAIAH 62:12

But of him are ye in Christ Jesus, who of God is made
unto us wisdom, and righteousness, and sanctification,
and redemption: that, according as it is written,
he that glorieth, let him glory in the Lord.
1 CORINTHIANS 1:30–31

That Christ may dwell in your hearts by faith;
that ye, being rooted and grounded in love, may be
able to comprehend with all saints what is the breadth,
and length, and depth, and height; and to know the
love of Christ, which passeth knowledge, that ye
might be filled with all the fulness of God.
EPHESIANS 3:17–19